CHATHAM HOUSE

D1100975

The Transformation of Western Europe

William Wallace

The Royal Institute of International Affairs

Pinter Publishers
London

First published in Great Britain in 1990 by
Pinter Publishers Limited
25 Floral Street, London WC2E 9DS

British Library Cataloguing in Publication Data

A CIP catalogue record for this book is available from the British Library

ISBN 0-86187-889-2 (Paperback)
     0-86187-116-2 (Hardback)

Reproduced from copy supplied by
Stephen Austin and Sons Ltd
Printed and bound in Great Britain by
Biddles Ltd

CONTENTS

Maps

ACKNOWLEDGMENTS

This paper stems from a collaborative study on long-term trends in European integration, which brought together some two dozen experts from different countries and disciplines for a series of working conferences in the course of 1988–9. The majority of the papers prepared in the course of that project will be published, in William Wallace, ed., *The Dynamics of European Integration,* later in 1990. This shorter essay draws on the detailed material which other contributors provided, on discussions within our three conferences in Ebenhausen, Brussels and Florence, and on comments on drafts presented to groups in Stockholm, the Hague and London.

I am grateful to all those who contributed advice, criticism, and their own research to this project; in particular to Philippe de Schouteete, Albert Bressand, Loukas Tsoukalis and Margaret Sharp, for active encouragement throughout and written comments on drafts. Reinhard Rummel helped to define the project, and was my host in Ebenhausen. Helen Wallace, as head of the Institute's West European Programme, was my formal supervisor, as well as a source of expert and constructive criticism from the original idea to the final manuscript. Michael Klein and Martin Spät provided statistics and references. Jane Pugh of the Cartographic Unit of the London School of Economics prepared the maps. Many other members of the Institute's staff provided comments, filled in gaps in my knowledge, and introduced me to relevant literature.

Financial support for the year's leave which enabled me to conduct this study came from the Thyssen Foundation, the (British) Economic and Social Research Council and the Royal Institute of International Affairs. Our successive working conferences were supported by the Thyssen Foundation, the Stiftung Wissenschaft und Politik, the Spaak Foundation, the Commission of the European Community, and the European University Institute.

February 1990   W.W.

1
INTRODUCTION AND SUMMARY

Political controversies often revolve round divergent assumptions about long-term trends. Are underlying patterns of industrial production, technological innovation, financial integration and social interchange undermining the foundations of European nation-states, or have national frameworks successfully adapted without losing their autonomy and legitimacy? Is the 'European Union' to which the Single European Act declares its commitment the same objective as that declared in the Treaties of Paris and Rome, or have developments over the intervening 30–40 years changed the quality both of what is possible and of what is desired? What has been the impact of shifts in Europe's economic balance? How far have the security considerations which predominated in the 1940s given way to economic imperatives in shaping European politics? Is the 'Europe' to which our political leaders refer the same Europe as that described by their predecessors of ten, 20, 30 or 40 years ago – let alone of 60, 80 or 100 years ago?

The illusion of stability disguises the gradual processes of change. When – as in the autumn of 1989 – apparent stability gives way to rapid political change, it is important to examine both the underlying continuities and the evolutionary trends which have helped to create the conditions for these political changes. Western Europe's postwar structure, it should be remembered, was *intended* to be provisional: to await the postwar settlement of Germany's future constitution and boundaries, and the internal transformation of a contained Soviet Union. Its stability over more than 40 years is

1

testimony both to the order imposed by nuclear deterrence and to the inability of the Europeans themselves – both West and East – to shake off their postwar dependence on their superpower patrons.

Political, economic and cultural developments follow different timescales.[1] In politics, long periods of stability alternate with intervals of rapid change: moving sometimes in decades, sometimes in weeks. Misled by the appearance of institutional stability, politicians of all countries tend to endow the status quo with an illusory permanence. So British opponents of entry to the European Community appealed to 'a thousand years of British history' in defence of a state united for barely 250 years and a concept of sovereignty (and of history) developed in the late nineteenth century. So, earlier, German nationalists asserted the permanence of a Reich which had emerged after centuries of disunity, to collapse after less than 50 years, and to be recreated for little more than a decade. The distinctive position of NATO has been that it has served at the same time to promote change and to maintain stability. The communiqués of NATO summits have ritually reaffirmed their determination to 'overcome ... the unnatural division of Europe, and particularly of Germany', as well as to see a more united Europe assuming a greater share 'of the risks, roles and responsibilities of the Atlantic partnership'.[2] But most of the signatories to such statements have carried away from such meetings implicit reservations about the objectives stated, and implicit expectations about the continuity of the West-West and East-West relationships they have inherited, which left them shaken by the implications of the rapid changes of late 1989, when the postwar security structure of Europe began to turn upside down.

The formal structures of the European Community were intended, in contrast, to be permanent: 'to create, by establishing an economic community, the basis for a broader and deeper community among peoples long divided by bloody conflicts; and to lay the foundations for institutions which will give direction to a destiny henceforward shared'.[3] Yet their persistence and consolidation have been accompanied almost since the outset by repeated preoccupation with enlargement of the membership and revision of the EC's powers and competences. Periods of optimism about the construction of a united Europe have alternated with intervals of pessimism about prospects for West European cooperation – as noted in Chapter 5. The 'European space' and 'European identity' of which politicians were speaking in the late 1980s differed both in geographical extent and in character from what many political leaders had envisaged in the 1950s. Yet the contrast which defenders of national sovereignty draw between the flimsy novelty of this institutionalized Europe and the solidity of the nation-state is easily exaggerated. Europe's nation-states, as Chapters 2 and 4 argue, are themselves relatively recent constructions, assuming their modern structure at most a century ago, and are affected by the same underlying economic, technical and social trends which are gradually reshaping Europe as a whole.

The pace of economic and technical change is both slower than the eruption of immediate political events and more continuous in its evolution. It moves at one level in business cycles, and at a more fundamental level in the long cycles of innovation and consolidation which accompany the development of widely applicable new materials and technologies. European recovery after World War II, as noted in Chapter 3, was partly a matter of rebuilding the heavy industries which had characterized the industrial world from the 1880s on, partly a matter of catching up with the Americans in the following 'wave' of mass production, electrification and the exploitation of the internal combustion engine.[4] Similarly, West European economic planners in the 1970s and 1980s have been preoccupied with the impact of new core technologies and materials, most immediately with the implications of microelectronics and with the challenge which American and Japanese advances in these technologies pose for European interests. While West European anxieties provided impetus for closer cooperation in the 1980s, the failure of East European economic planners to appreciate or adapt to this shift in industrial dynamics contributed to the loss of confidence throughout the socialist world, and to the consequent turn towards their Western neighbours for the technology, capital and management skills needed to replace their outdated heavy industries.

Social and cultural changes follow yet other timescales. The social evolution of Europe since 1945 has been marked by rising interaction across frontiers, under the impulse of radio, television, motorways and charter aircraft; while the impact of communication on attitudes has been delayed by the slow passage of assumptions from one generation to another, and limited in its geographical spread by the physical boundary between West and East. Its cultural evolution has been marked by a pronounced Americanization, or globaliza-

3

tion, of popular tastes. But it has been marked as well by a persistent desire, on the part of intellectuals and politicians, to differentiate between 'Europe' and 'America', which has found an echo in popular attitudes. Underneath the Atlantic framework of the post-war West European order have lain cultural and historical images from previous eras – of central Europe, of Western Christendom, of 'the West' – which still shape responses to developments in Poland and Hungary, Bulgaria and Turkey. History and identity go together, both at the national and at the European level. The re-emergence of older historical frames of reference from beneath the overlay of the cold war has been one of the most significant European political developments of the 1980s, throwing up some awkward issues of definition and redefinition for policy-makers in the 1990s.

The aim of this paper is to examine the interaction between political, economic and social trends in Western Europe. It draws upon a larger collaborative study undertaken in the course of 1988–9, which set out to investigate the changing shape of Western Europe *not* from Brussels outwards but from observed patterns of trade, travel, and communication.[5] It does *not* assume, as committed supporters of European union have often assumed, that the European Community defines or determines Western Europe, but that the importance of its various institutional structures and the cohesiveness of Western Europe as a region are themselves proper subjects for investigation. We therefore looked at the Atlantic Alliance and Western European Union, the Organization for Economic Cooperation and Development and the Council of Europe, and the many other *ad hoc* organizations through which the governments of Western Europe collaborate, as well as at the European Community. The balance between political-military relations, institutionalized within an Atlantic framework, and political-economic relations, institutionalized partly on an Atlantic basis and partly within Western Europe, indeed emerged as one of the underlying questions of the study.

Questions such as these rarely lend themselves to any definitive answers. The evidence available in almost all areas is insufficient and open to different interpretations; accidental events, persuasive political leadership or external pressures intervene to disrupt neat patterns and alter trends. But it is nevertheless possible to expose some of the issues which are trampled underfoot in the cut and thrust of political bargaining and the clash of contradictory perspectives. A great many features of Europe's political, economic, security and social environment were in movement at the end of the 1980s. Uncertainty about future direction coexisted with commitment to established institutions and aims. The mental maps which have guided West European leaders for the last three or four decades were being challenged, both by the re-emergence of the old maps of historical Europe and by the imagery of the global market and of the Pacific as an alternative focus to the Atlantic. The 1990s may well see radical changes. Assessment of the likely direction and pace of change should start from a review of the dynamics of change in the 1960s and 1970s – and from a recognition that the established order of the late 1980s has evolved a long way from the order which was established in the years after World War II.

Chapter 2 sets the context within which the development of Europe must be discussed, by exploring the different definitions of 'Europe' as an historical, geographical, economic, political and cultural entity, and the underpinnings of symbols and values which are inseparable from any concept of Europe. It notes the overlap between concepts of Western Europe and of Europe as such, linked by the old distinction between Europe as 'the West' and Asia as 'the East'; and argues that Western Europe – defined in the postwar sense to include the greater part of Germany – is the political and economic core of Europe, as it has been (with successive alterations in internal balance) for many centuries. Chapter 3 sketches the transformation of Western Europe since the end of World War II and the construction of the postwar political order. Chapter 4 steps back again to examine the dynamics of political, economic and social integration which have shaped European (and global) developments over the past century. Chapter 5 reconsiders the processes of change in Western Europe since the political 'project' of European union was launched in the years immediately after World War II, tracing the interaction between political ideals, security considerations, economic and technical developments, and social evolution. Chapter 6 discusses the likely direction of future developments in Europe in the light of the trends identified and the institutional structures erected to manage them.

The argument of this volume is that Western Europe has been defined and secured for the past 40 years by institutional structures provided by its American protector and patron – with the sharp boundary between Western and Eastern Europe defined by Soviet hostility. Within that wider protected space the integration of Western Europe has developed (with the encouragement of the United States) around a core area, which has progressively drawn other economies and societies – and therefore governments – towards it. A stable American-led political and institutional framework has allowed for a gradual transformation of economic and social interaction within Western Europe, which has in turn created pressures for institutional adjustments to manage the cross-border flows. The impetus for further formal – institutional – integration in the 1980s has derived more from these economic, technical and social changes than from the political and security objectives which drove the initial construction.

The politics of Western Europe have been guided for 40 years by a generation for which World War II constituted the formative political period and reference point. That generation is now passing out of active politics. Presidents Reagan and Bush, Margaret Thatcher, François Mitterrand and Giulio Andreotti were at the end of the 1980s the last Western political leaders for whom the war and its immediate aftermath were matters of direct personal involvement or recollection. The postwar political generation which was by then succeeding them had grown up through the transformation of Europe from postwar deprivation to affluence, without experiencing the forces which gave the West European space we live in its shape. In 1990 those born after 1945 constitute a clear majority of Europe's current population; by 2000 they will constitute a clear majority of its voters. The political assumptions and historical context which underpin the institutional structures of Europe are thus likely to be less and less widely understood – or shared – by both politicians and publics as the 1990s progress.

Changes in Western Europe's international environment, together with the magnetic attraction of core Western Europe for its neighbours, are now shaking the stability of the postwar political framework which has fostered its growth, opening up some underlying questions about the institutional structure, political identity and boundaries of Western Europe. This essay examines the historical context from which to address those questions: the 'Where did we start from?', 'How did we get here?', 'Where did we think we were going?', and 'Where are we now?', which are the necessary preliminaries to 'Where should we go from here?'

2
EUROPE, WHICH EUROPE?

'Europe' is a geographical expression with political significance and immense symbolic weight, but without clear definition or agreed boundaries. 'The word "Europe" has been used and misused, interpreted and misinterpreted, in as many different meanings as almost any word in any language.'[1] Article 237 of the Treaty of Rome states that 'Any European State may apply to become a member of the European Community.' It has therefore mattered to the governments of post-Franco Spain and post-'colonels' Greece, as in the 1980s it mattered to the governments of Turkey and Malta, whether they were considered by their neighbours to be included in the accepted definition of Europe. Such concepts as 'European values', 'European solidarity', 'European security' and 'European culture' are freely used in political debate in many countries, though rarely defined. The identification of a European company, or of 'European content' in manufactured goods, is subject to legal definition and administrative measurement. But the 'common European home' of Mr Gorbachev's rhetoric is an imagined space, as have been so many of the 'Europes' to which political leaders have appealed – for highly divergent political motives – over many centuries.

Mental maps, imagined space, define political regions and communities.[2] Such broad concepts as 'the West' or 'the Orient' cover no well-delineated territories; their appeal is in the associations they conjure up, mixing geographical space with economic and social interaction and with political and cultural identity to draw an imaginary – but nevertheless effectively recognized – divide. So, similarly, with Europe and its constituent imagined regions, northern and southern, East, Central and West. 'Central Europe is not a region whose boundaries you can trace on the map – like, say, Central America. It is a kingdom of the spirit':[3] a region created by intellectuals to persuade others to think about their relations with their neighbours in a particular way. It is the task of the politician and the lawyer, more than of the geographer or the economist, to reduce such loosely defined spaces to precise and bounded territories. The boundaries of Europe are a matter of politics and of ideology: Russia, Turkey, Spain under Franco and since, Yugoslavia, Romania or Albania under their different regimes, may be included or excluded according to the definition preferred.

The concept of Europe has shifted significantly during the 1980s. 'It can safely be asserted that a person who had learnt his geography and history as recently as twenty years ago would be more often than not at a loss to comprehend the continental events recorded in our daily papers' – as Karl Polanyi wrote 50 years ago, but could as easily remark today.[4] The space conventionally referred to on both sides of the Atlantic as 'Europe' for 30 years has again become 'Western Europe': though a rather different Western Europe from what was understood 50 or 100 years ago. The region conventionally defined for the past 40 years as Eastern Europe is now a contested area, with intellectuals and governments rediscovering and redefining central Europe and east-central Europe, pushing their imagined dividing lines to the east to group themselves with their western neighbours and leave the Soviet Union, with its constituent republics, on its own.

The observer – or the politician – may attempt to define Europe in several ways. The most straightforward is in terms of institutional and political structure; though even this leaves us with several alternatives. There has been a tendency since the optimistic years of the 1960s to identify 'Europe' with the member states of the European Community: those whose governments had declared their commitment to build a 'European union', resting upon a common sense of 'European identity' and a shared 'European idea'.[5] Thus politicians outside the European Community would call on their governments to 'join Europe', while those of opposing views would accept the label 'anti-European'.[6] Committed 'Europeans' adjusted their definitions of European culture and identity to fit its changing institutional contours each time the Community was enlarged.

There was, of course, a broader institutional 'Europe' from the earliest postwar years; defined by the closely linked memberships of the OEEC/OECD and the Council of Europe. These, too, expanded gradually: from the original 16 national delegations which set up the Committee of European Economic Cooperation in 1947 to the 19 European members of the present OECD (adding Federal Germany, then occupied territory, Finland and Spain); from the 10 signatories of the Statute of the Council of Europe in 1949 (the five Brussels Treaty signatories, plus Denmark, Norway, Sweden, Ireland and Italy) to the 23 members of 40 years later. Acceptance of the obligations of membership also defined a certain conception of Europe: market economies and liberal/constitutional systems of government were conditions of inclusion. The 'European Economic Space' constituted in the 1980s by the enlarged EC and the six EFTA countries thus represented a broad political community, with the Mediterranean members of the Council of Europe and the OECD clinging to its coat-tails (see Map 1). But there is also the institutionalized Europe of the Atlantic security system: the 'European Pillar' of the Atlantic Alliance, with the seven member governments of Western European Union (increased to nine by the accession of Spain and Portugal in 1988) as its core.

The broader 'Europe' defined by the United Nations' plans for postwar reconstruction and cooperation faded as the cold war intensified, leaving the UN Economic Commission for Europe as an almost empty shell. Detente in the 1970s led to institutional revival, most significantly in the '35-nation' Conference on Security and Cooperation in Europe; though this included not only the USA and Canada, extra-European states with forces in place on the European continent, but also such micro-states as Liechtenstein and the Vatican. With such broad interpretations of Europe as a region, rather than as a bounded area marked by the acceptance of common obligations, we come up against the problem of drawing any outside limits to 'Europe'. The participating states within the CSCE, after all, stretch from Vancouver to Vladivostok.

Alternatively, one may attempt to define Europe in terms of history, or historical geography; or in terms of observed patterns of social, economic and political interaction; or in terms of values,

Map 1 The European economic space

culture, and psychological identity – or perceived community. The first is a happy hunting ground for intellectual dispute; the second a more straightforward task for empirical research; and the third the most subjective and contentious territory of all. All three definitions, however, feed into the evolution of European politics: the first as a source of symbolic associations and identifications; the second as a focus for policy, and as a process which builds patterns of mutual identification and community; the third as an area for political and ideological conflict both in European international politics and within the domestic politics of European states.

Historical Europes
'History', as the Soviet negotiator remarks in *A Walk in the Woods*,

'is only geography stretched over time.'[7] Until the mid-1980s the apparent solidity of the geopolitical barrier between the Atlantic Alliance and the Warsaw Pact suggested that the politically relevant historical frame of reference could safely be limited to the past 40 years; though the acceptance of Greece into a European Community which had until then been entirely 'Western' in extent demonstrated the political potency of far earlier points of reference, and the reassertion of Spain's European links after the death of General Franco also reasserted older patterns.[8] Western Europe was part of the Atlantic world of 'Euramerica' (see Map 2). The rusting of the iron curtain has, however, led to the vigorous reassertion – in the politics of the late 1980s – of the relevance of earlier Europes: above all the European society and political system of the nineteenth century and the interwar years, but also the worlds of Western Christendom, the Renaissance and the European Enlightenment.

The historian who sets out to write on the development of Europe unavoidably imposes his own assumptions on the tangle of evidence with which he is faced. Nineteenth-century historians, German, British, French or Italian, were not shy of using history to point the moral for the present: to demonstrate the centrality of Germany, the exceptional position and experience of Britain, the civilizing mission of France, or the imperial contributions of Rome. Most saw themselves as national historians, tracing the evolution of their 'nation's story' to reinforce the sense of national identity. But there were others, liberal idealists and cosmopolitans, who set out to demonstrate the essential unity of European experience, in order to argue for greater solidarity among the separate nations of Europe: each party interpreting the past to justify its preferred strategy for the present. There were indeed many idealistic nationalists, like Mazzini, who saw a united Europe emerging out of the replacement of its patchwork of states and empires by free and self-governing nations.[9]

The political, economic, cultural and human expansion of Europe in the course of the nineteenth century complicated definition further. North America, Australasia and Argentina became extensions of Europe; many other countries in South America, as well as eastern and southern Africa, were lands of European settlement and domination. 'Europeanization' and 'modernization' were synonymous for states which wished to catch up with France, Britain, and later Germany, as these three countries competed for

11

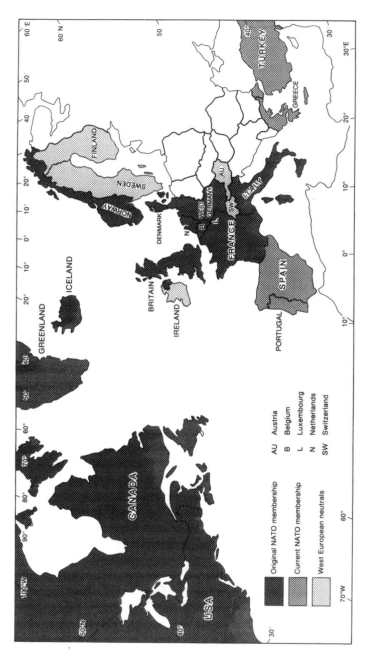

Map 2 Euramerica

political, economic and cultural superiority. First Peter the Great's Russia, then post-Meiji restoration Japan, then Kemal Ataturk's Turkey, saw the adoption of European education and institutions, and even of European dress, manners, dancing styles, as the key to national advance. In the confident decades which preceded World War I, European history and world history seemed practically synonymous; 'the expansion of Europe' (the title of many world history courses in European universities as late as the 1970s) was the march of progress.

Nevertheless one can distil out of the tide of European historiography a stream of development which is of relevance to the assumptions and uncertainties which underlie current policy. Europe as a region has never had clear boundaries. But it has had identifiable core areas, shifting slowly over time in response to internal and external developments. In the ancient world the northern shores of the Mediterranean constituted the core area, stretching northwards and southwards for trade and political control. Barbarian incursions from the north-east divided the Roman world. The explosion of Arab power in the early years of Islam pushed the principalities of what had by then become Western Christendom north and west, with the Arab conquest of Spain and Arab incursions across the Mediterranean. The economic core of medieval Europe – which is to say, its richest and most densely populated area – ran from Bruges and the merchant cities of Flanders through Burgundy, the Rhineland, southern Germany and the Alpine passes to Milan, Genoa, Florence and Venice. Outwards from there the Hanseatic towns traded with the peripheral regions of the north, and the Italian cities developed and controlled the trade with the East, in conflict but also in limited cooperation with the Byzantine empire and the Arab world.

Discovery of alternative routes to trade with the Indies, and alternative sources of wealth in the new American empires, tilted the balance of advantage away from the Mediterranean countries to those which bordered the ocean: first Spain and Portugal, then England and the Netherlands. The mouth of the Rhine, rather than the slopes of the Alps, became the major route to and from the rich cities of the Holy Roman empire. The shift of balance north and west was sharpened by parallel external and internal factors: the vigorous expansion of the Turkish empire, occupying most of the Hungarian kingdom after the battle of Mohacs in 1526, leaving

Austria as the eastern bastion of the Christian West; the Turkish naval expansion which followed, dominating the Mediterranean and bringing the whole of North Africa under Turkish suzerainty; the religious wars following the Reformation, which devastated and impoverished much of Germany, as well as Flanders, leaving France (which came out of its civil wars with a strong central government), England and the Netherlands as the leading powers in the early eighteenth century.

It is a common theme of European economic and political history that the fragmentation of the territories of the Holy Roman empire played a crucial role in Europe's development. Free cities and prosperous small states promoted trade and industry, and acted as a barrier to attempts to impose the deadweight of imperial centralization.[10] The dispersal of political authority in western and southern Germany and in Italy survived the Hapsburg attempt to assert imperial dominance. It allowed the brief Swedish attempt to create a northern empire, and the much more sustained French efforts to establish a dominant position both in northern Italy and in the Rhineland. The role which German forces played in the struggle for dominance inside and outside Europe between Britain and France in the course of the eighteenth century is obscured in the national histories of both those countries by considering only the parts played by Austria and Prussia, leaving out of account the Hanoverians and Brunswickers who constituted one-third of Wellington's army at Waterloo, or the troops from Bavaria, Baden and the Rhineland who marched with Napoleon to Moscow.

Yet from the medieval period on, the loose grouping of peoples who came to call themselves Germans have constituted the largest single entity in Christian Europe. They spilled across the central areas of European society and the European economy, without defined or settled boundaries. The early German emperors held their court in Aachen. Their successors moved progressively east from the Rhineland to Goslar and the Harz mountains, to Bamberg and Swabia, and on to Regensburg and Worms. The Emperor Charles IV used Prague as his capital; the later Hapsburgs ruled from Vienna. As the Swiss cantons and the Low Countries detached themselves, so Pomerania and Silesia were incorporated. Throughout northern and eastern Europe, trade and towns developed with German settlement, as German artisans and merchants moved into the Slav lands, making German the dominant language of commerce and – except for the period of the French Enlightenment – of culture.

The fragmentation of authority within the German territories left space for France's bid for European dominance, and for Britain's subsequent leading role. The industrial pre-eminence of Britain in the early nineteenth century reinforced the westward tilt of European wealth and power. Industrialization spread across Europe from west to east, from Britain to Belgium, northern France, the Rhineland, and northern Italy, and from there to pockets of industry in Eastern Europe.[11] The unification of most of the German territories under Prussian leadership owed something to the experience of French dominance, which roused a sense of German nationalism, and something to the experience of Britain's industrial supremacy, which led to the *Zollverein*.

Once unification was achieved, after the Franco-Prussian war of 1870–72, the dominance of imperial Germany in continental Europe, in population, resources, trade and investment was rapidly established – as J.M. Keynes noted in surveying the damage to Europe's economic balance, threatened by the terms of the Versailles Treaty of 1919. 'Round Germany as a central support the rest of the European economic system grouped itself, and on the prosperity and enterprise of Germany the prosperity of the rest of the Continent mainly depended.' In the decade before World War I the German empire was the first trading partner of Russia, Norway, Sweden, Denmark, Belgium, Switzerland, Italy and Austria-Hungary; and the second for Great Britain and France. German investment and capital goods flowed most strongly to Russia, Austria-Hungary, Romania, Bulgaria and Turkey. 'The whole of Europe east of the Rhine thus fell into the German industrial orbit, and its economic life was adjusted accordingly.'[12]

Historical boundaries, modern boundaries

This brief delineation of the evolution of modern Europe is intended to emphasize the extent to which the core areas of economic, cultural and political development in modern Europe have lain in what we now call Western Europe. The approximate coincidence of the 'little Europe' of the Six with Charlemagne's reconstituted western 'Roman empire' (see map 3) even led some enthusiasts in the 1950s and 1960s to exaggerate the degree of historical continuity, disregarding the abrupt and artificial eastern boundary which the cold

Map 3 The political core of Europe

war had by then imposed.[13] Political and economic developments in eastern Europe had been limited by the greater dispersion of population, and disrupted by invasions from the east and south-east. The Mongol invasions of the thirteenth century swept over Poland and Hungary to the edge of the German lands, before disunity weakened their armies; leaving Russia a tributary state under Tartar suzerainty for over 200 years.

The boundaries of Europe were defined by geography to the west and the north; to the east and south they moved forwards and backwards with conquest and reconquest. The Ottoman empire absorbed Bulgaria in the 1390s, Serbia and most of Bosnia – and the last pockets of the Byzantine empire – in the 1450s. In the 1520s the Turks conquered Hungary and threatened Austria; they continued to threaten Austria until the failure of the great siege of 1683. The seventeenth-century European system was thus, in modern terms, a West European system. The rise of Prussia and of Russia in the eighteenth century, and the beginnings of Turkish decline, brought Eastern Europe back in. Russia *became* a European power during this century, with its new capital on its western coast in St Petersburg, with French as a court language, Germans to organize its commerce, and Scots and Irish serving with its armies. The Russian court played an active part in the shifting alliance politics of eighteenth-century Europe, taking over the roles (and much of the territories) previously occupied by Sweden and Poland. Its troops fought Frederick the Great and Napoleon, and occupied both Berlin (in 1760) and Paris (with other allied troops, in 1814).

Historical definition of Europe began with its differentiation from Asia: a distinction which has faded into the subconscious on Europe's western edge, but which is still felt and asserted as one moves south and east. In medieval Europe the concept of Europe became interchangeable with that of Christendom: or rather, of western Christendom (see map 4). The conflict with Islam served briefly to unify the quarrelling princes of Western Europe in successive crusades, with the profitable distraction of attacking also Orthodox Byzantium. The Emperor Charles V failed to rally the newly Protestant princes within Germany against the Turkish armies, though in the Mediterranean cooperation among the Catholic powers overcame Turkish naval power. These layers of differentiation – between Protestant northern and Catholic southern Europe, between the countries of the Western tradition and those of the Orthodox world, and between the Christian world and Islam – have left imagined boundaries which persist today, deeply embedded in European history and literature from Metternich to Thomas Mann.[14] History here feeds directly into current politics and values, with Austrians protesting their prior right to Community entry over Turkey, and the Secretary-General of the Serbian Communist Party declaring that 'On Kosovo, as 600 years ago, the battle for Europe is being fought' against the forces of militant Islam.[15]

Each claimant to full European participation attempts to draw the boundaries of Europe around and behind it: to include all the countries of the Western tradition, of Catholicism and the Enlightenment, for Austria, Hungary and Poland; of the broader Christian tradition, for the southern republics of Yugoslavia,

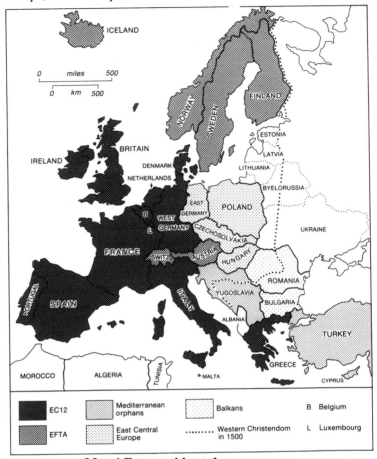

Map 4 Europe without the superpowers

Romania, Bulgaria and Russia; of the secularizing and modernizing tradition, for Turkey. Throughout the 1950s and 1960s Israeli governments similarly emphasized their place within the European tradition and region, pursuing Greece and Turkey in seeking association with the EC, actively participating in the party internationals, even joining in the Eurovision song contest (where it remains, together with Yugoslavia, Turkey and Cyprus, alongside the 18 members of EC and EFTA). A subsequent shift in political sentiment and generations reoriented Israeli self-identification away from Europe to the other side of the Atlantic. Each group of claimants except Turkey and Russia, it should be noted, is as concerned to *exclude* those beyond as to *include* themselves within the community of Europe: Hungarians, Czechs and Poles to shut out Russia; Serbs and Bulgarians to emphasize their distinctiveness from their Islamic neighbours; Israelis to stress the divide between 'Judaeo-Christian civilization' and Islam. Turkey and Russia thus represent Europe's outer limits, each uncomfortably aware that its case for inclusion is not conclusive. If Russia, why not America? If Turkey, why not Morocco, Algeria, Tunisia?

The successful re-establishment of the nation-state across Western Europe in the years after World War II has obscured the contingent quality – even the artificiality – of Europe's current boundaries and of the national myths which support them. In Europe, east and west, in 1989 there were only ten states which retained substantially the same boundaries as they had had in 1899, and of these Spain was the only sizeable country. The United Kingdom has lost most of Ireland since then; France has regained (and lost, and regained) Alsace and Lorraine, but lost its North African departments. The states of Eastern Europe emerged out of the collapse of the German, Russian and Austro-Hungarian empires in 1918; to be redrawn, with massive shifts of population, in 1945. The history of Europe, and the myths which apologists have created to support it, remains a contested area. But so does the history of Spain, and of Belgium, and of Germany – and even of the United Kingdom.[16]

In one sense European history ended in World War II, with the partition of Europe into Atlantic and Soviet systems. The expansion of Europe across the Atlantic in the course of the nineteenth century had created an alternative – or complementary – history to which writers and politicians could appeal. The *History of the English-Speaking Peoples* conjured up an Atlantic and maritime world, of which Europe was only a minor part.[17] 'The Atlantic idea' stressed the common experience, and values, which Western Europe shared with North America, of capitalism and democracy: an experience which only Czechoslovakia and the GDR from behind the iron curtain had shared to any significant degree.[18] Under the pressures of the cold war, West European perceptions of natural linkages shifted. Louis Halle points out that the style of map projections and even the classification of ornithological species reflected this shift from a broad European to an Atlantic perspective, which indicates that 'geography is conceptual as much as physical.'[19] As the cold war receded, other conceptual maps re-emerged, drawing on alternative perspectives of history and geography. 'We believed', a leading Hungarian historian wrote in the early 1980s of the Hungarian experience of the 1940s, 'that [the great tenth-century Magyar leader] Arpad had posted us in the West, separating us once and for all from the eastern nations among which we had grown into an independent nation; now we have realised that ... Eurasia reached out for us again.'[20] Russia is thus identified with the East, the 'Asiatic' model of production and government; Western Europe with the 'West' and with all that flowed from the development of European civilization out of Western Christendom.

Buried underneath the rhetoric and imagery of the cold war, of Atlantic solidarity and the free world, lay another politico-geographical concept: that of Europe as an entity separate and distinct from the two great powers which flanked it to the east and west. The concept of a European region which was culturally and politically separate both from Soviet Eurasia and from capitalist Euramerica was subversive of both alliance systems, conjuring up a 'third force' in a bipolar world: a romantic idea for Gaullists and democratic socialists, but not legitimate in the harsh climate of postwar confrontation. The cold war's renewed exclusion of the countries east of Germany from interaction with their Western neighbours only reinforced the strength of the belief 'in the reality, and the importance, of a European cultural community ... within the countries lying between EEC territory and the Soviet Union.'[21] But that raises questions of identity and values, to which we will return later.

The postwar politicians who set out to 'build Europe' worked, as we have noted, within the framework set by Russian hostility and American sponsorship. They were, it appears, less concerned to describe the outer boundaries of their imagined Europe than to organize the countries at its core. Monnet's core Europe consisted of France, Britain and Germany. The last of these entities was itself loosely defined; there were many in Western Europe in the 1940s who retained a sense of distinction between the Rhineland, Prussia, and the regions in between, and were happy to see the distinctions re-emerge as political boundaries. The thrust of Monnet's strategy until 1950 was to bring these three countries into a closer union; thereafter, to bring France and Germany together in the hope and expectation that Britain would be drawn into that union once it was created.

The Benelux countries had no choice but to participate in such an enterprise, given their high dependence on Germany and France; the postwar Italian government was determined to assert its European commitment and to rebuild its economic and political links with the democracies of Western Europe. Beyond these – the countries of the European movement's core Europe (and of the American administration's core Europe) – the political and economic stakes were lower. The smaller countries of the periphery were to be welcomed, if they would join; but their presence was not essential to the enterprise.[22]

Patterns of interaction: core and periphery in contemporary Europe
We are on firmer ground if we define Europe, as Karl Deutsch would define a political community, by measuring the intensity of communication among its different units, bearing in mind that the framework of formal rules and boundaries shapes and directs the flow. Western Europe is a densely populated, geographically compact area. The population of the Twelve is 140% that of the USA, but occupies a territory only one-quarter the size of the American. The EC's most densely populated regions are grouped along the same axis from the Low Countries to northern Italy as in medieval Europe: the Netherlands and North-Rhine-Westphalia, with some 500 people per square kilometre, are the most tightly packed.[23] The intensity of interaction within the core area of the Rhine valley, south-eastern England, northern France, and over the Alpine passes into northern Italy is a matter for comment only because the barriers imposed by national frontiers and controls had earlier interrupted the flow. The territory covered is after all comparable in size only with the north-east corner of the United States, and the borders between France and Germany, Belgium and the Netherlands are almost entirely arbitrary and artificial.

The United States operated for almost 100 years without a clearly defined western frontier, its population, its economy, its laws spreading as it grew. The European region is already fully occupied by organized states. But it may nevertheless be useful to think of economic and social Europe – and to some extent also of political Europe – in terms of an organized core and a dependent periphery, the influence and magnetic attraction of the core spreading as it develops. The economists' definition of a core area is of a region which exports advanced industrial goods, services and capital, and imports labour, semi-manufactures and raw materials; its dominant relationship with its peripheral regions is marked by disparities of wealth and by imbalances in transactions.[24] Where political and institutional conditions allow, the flow of capital and technology out from the established core to new areas, as in the nineteenth-century European economy, leads to a gradual expansion of the 'economic space', involving a shift in the balance of advantage as new industries and services grow up in different regions to challenge the old.[25]

The most striking – and obvious – point to emerge from the briefest glance at economic, social and political flows across European national boundaries is the massive discontinuity which has been represented by the East-West divide, and the comparative unimportance of the boundary between EC membership and non-membership in interactions across OECD Europe. Federal Germany, it is true, has been throughout the 1980s the second trade partner after the Soviet Union for all the countries of CMEA Europe (the Council for Mutual Economic Assistance, popularly known as Comecon); but total CMEA trade, excluding the special relationship with East Germany, accounted in 1986 for only 3.5% of the FRG's foreign trade – less than that with Norway or Portugal. CMEA Europe has become, even more than in the Europe of before World War I, peripheral Europe, separate from but dependent upon its Western neighbours. This is as evident in culture and communications as in trade. Broadcasts of West German (and/or Austrian) television have reached almost all the GDR, and parts of western Poland and Czechoslovakia, for many years, outweighing official channels. Western radio has been listened to throughout Eastern Europe; including those Atlantic hybrids, Radio Liberty and Radio Free Europe, funded and controlled by the US government but based in Germany and staffed largely by Europeans from both east and west of the central divide.

The patterns of trade which have evolved since European economies recovered from World War II provide the most striking evidence of a European region focused around a dynamic core area. They also supply clear evidence of the importance of politics and trade policy, of boundaries and rules, in shaping economic flows. The European economy of the early twentieth century, as described by J.M. Keynes, was one in which German economic links stretched most strongly east and south-east: to Russia, Austria-Hungary, Bulgaria, Romania and Turkey, in which group of countries half of Germany's accumulated foreign investments had been placed.[26] The countries west and south-west of Germany, Britain and France, Spain and Portugal, had a lower degree of mutual economic dependence with this imperial Germany, trading across the Atlantic and with their maritime empires. Eastern and south-eastern Europe constituted, in effect, a dependent periphery of this core German economy: its dependent relationship reinforced by high tariffs and politically motivated trade and investment 'concessions'.

The (West) European economy which had developed within the OEEC framework by the late 1950s revolved around two pivotal economies: that of Germany, with high mutual economic dependence on its western, southern and northern neighbours, and of Britain, on which the Scandinavian countries of the newly created EFTA depended more heavily than on Germany. These were Western Europe's two largest economies, and around them the six-nation EC and the seven-nation EFTA were built – with the anomaly that the two Alpine neutral states, Austria and Switzerland, were economically linked to the Six, which absorbed 54% of Austria's exports and 42% of Switzerland's, but for political reasons attached themselves to the looser association. Forty per cent of Denmark's exports, 37% of Norway's, and 36% of Sweden's went to their Scandinavian neighbours and to Britain, constituting a pattern of economic interaction in which Britain was the strongest pole of attraction, with Sweden as a secondary focus. Sweden was, indeed, Britain's third largest European trading partner in 1958, not far behind West Germany and Ireland, and well ahead of France and Italy.

'Economic integration is a dynamic process, in which one step invites another. Creation of a trading bloc changes the competitive position of outsiders and sets up pressures for further change.'[27] Increasing concentration of trade upon other European partners during the 1960s and 1970s was accompanied by the gradual enlargement of the EC and the strengthening of the centrality of the core area constituted by the German economy, the Low Countries, northern France, and to a lesser extent the Alpine countries and northern Italy; and was followed by the regularization of a closer formal relationship between the EFTA Six and the EC Twelve in what Community jargon of the mid-1980s labelled the 'European Economic Space'. Of the 18 countries of the EC and EFTA in 1987, only four (Iceland, Switzerland, Finland and the United Kingdom) sent as much as one-third of their national exports outside the space

23

thus defined. The UK and France, which as imperial powers had retained an extra-European trade orientation in the 1950s, had substantially reoriented their economic links towards their European neighbours: from 30% of exports to 57% for the UK, from 39% to 65% for France.[28]

The core position of the German economy in the integrated European economy of the 1980s is evident. It was the most important trading partner of all its immediate western and southern neighbours, and had long since displaced Britain as a partner in Scandinavian trade. It was the most important supplier to the Italian, Spanish, Portuguese, Greek, Yugoslav and Turkish markets, the second most important supplier (after the Soviet Union) to the CMEA countries of Eastern Europe and (after Italy or France) to Cyprus, Malta, Tunisia, and Libya – the centre of a broader regional network which now included a highly dependent periphery.[29]

The pattern of financial interactions was more diffuse. Western Europe in the late 1980s contained several financial centres: London and Zurich competing with Paris, Frankfurt, Luxembourg and Amsterdam. Swiss, German and British international banks were being challenged by French and Dutch – and all were facing increasing competition from American and Japanese financial houses as these established themselves in European markets. The core 'area of density of financial transactions' now stretched 'from Great Britain over the Benelux countries, France and Germany to Switzerland'.[30] The importance of Switzerland in financial core Europe was indicated by the extensive use of the Swiss franc as a vehicle currency in the inter-bank and Eurobond markets, challenging the D-mark for second place behind the dollar; and also by the regular meetings of the Committee of Central Bank Governors in Basle – the only organ of the European Community which normally meets outside its territorial boundaries.

The weight of the German economy had, however, carried the D-mark – and with it the Bundesbank – into a dominant position in international exchange markets as a point of reference and a reserve currency. This was already evident in the late 1960s, with the devaluation of sterling in 1967 and the subsequent erosion of the pound's international role, and the devaluation of the French franc against the D-mark in 1969. French proposals for economic and monetary union, accepted by the six heads of government at the Hague summit of December 1969 and developed into the 1970

24

Werner Plan, stemmed from the recognition that the West German currency – and economy – had now become the driving force within the EC. The 'snake' of jointly floating European currencies which followed associated the Swedish and Norwegian currencies with those of the enlarging EC; though the European Monetary System which, in 1979, succeeded the snake was limited to EC member states. The centrality of the D-mark in European and global international exchange markets became increasingly apparent in the 1980s, with the D-mark serving as the primary link between the EMS currencies, the dollar and the yen.

Patterns of investment flows, of ownership and of industrial integration also indicate a diffuse network of interconnections within a wider core area. Britain, France and Germany have been both the main suppliers and the main European recipients of international investment flows throughout the 1980s, interacting with the United States and Japan as well as with other European countries. The Netherlands has been the major player of the second rank, with Sweden and Switzerland expanding their positions as bases for Europe-wide companies. Institutional obstacles inhibited the growth of foreign investment in Italy, though some Italian companies were emerging as major European enterprises. Conversely, Spanish integration into the European economy was accelerated by encouragement of inward investment, locking Spanish production of automobiles and aerospace components into integrated European networks. Investment and entrepreneurial expansion was also converting some Norwegian and Finnish enterprises into Europe-wide companies, making for a pattern of economic integration which bore less relation to the formal boundaries of the EC than to the spread of wealth and accumulated investment capital within the European economic space.[31]

The impression that West Germany may be taken as 'the proxy for Western Europe as a whole, since the entire region's growth performance depends heavily on Germany's' is strengthened when we look at technological advance.[32] According to one recent study, 40% of all European patents applied for in 1985 originated in Germany, with France in second place and Britain, the Netherlands and Italy following behind.[33] The European defence industry sector in the 1980s possessed 'a core and a periphery in a double sense': a core of countries, the UK, France and Germany, and in some sectors also Italy, and a core of large companies within those countries which through a series of mergers and strategic alliances was becoming much more concentrated in 1988–9.[34]

The pattern of social interaction is remarkably similar, being one of extensive interaction around a core area. As a rich and densely populated country, Germany spills over onto the territories of its neighbours, in tourism and in second home ownership. OECD figures indicate that in 1986 Germans made twice as many tourist journeys to other parts of OECD Europe as nationals of any other country: 40m as against 20m for Britain and 11m for the Netherlands and for France.[35] German tourists were the predominant visitors in Austria, Switzerland, France, the Netherlands, Italy, Yugoslavia and Turkey; they were also the largest national group of Western visitors to East European countries. German ownership of second homes was a sensitive political issue in Denmark and Austria, and a recognized presence in Ireland, Spain and Italy. Along the European coasts of the Mediterranean, colonies of residents from northern Europe were growing. In 1986, 35,000 of the foreign residents in Spain were from West Germany, together with 50,000 from Britain, 12,000 from the Netherlands, and 5,500 from Sweden.

The core countries of Europe exported tourists and imported labour. In the 1950s and 1960s migrant workers flowed into the core regions of Western Europe from Spain, Portugal, southern Italy, Yugoslavia, Greece and Turkey – and in the north from Finland to Sweden. In the 1970s and 1980s as the prosperous core expanded many of these flows were reversed. The magnetic attraction of West European prosperity was now pulling in labour from a wider periphery: from Eastern Europe into Germany and Sweden, from North Africa into Italy, France and Spain, and from further parts of Asia into Germany, the Low Countries and Scandinavia. Some of these came officially as refugees; others came across the Mediterranean as illegal immigrants. Unofficial estimates indicated that there were 1.25m unregistered migrants in Italy in 1988, and 750,000 in Spain, most from the Muslim countries of North Africa.

It is harder to trace the emergence of mutual flows among the core countries of Western Europe, suggesting the beginnings of an imagined 'European social space' within which young workers, rising professionals and senior managers moved increasingly freely. Freedom of movement under the Treaty of Rome both facilitates such movement and makes it harder for the observer to obtain accurate statistics. 'Specific studies on transfer of managerial and professional workers indicate a steady intra-European movement, a strong attraction by Germany and ... the growing role of intra-company transfers'; most markedly among Germany, France, the Benelux countries, Denmark and Britain, but also including Sweden and Switzerland.[36]

Statistics on student movements are more readily available. Until the early 1980s the USA was the first foreign destination for West European students, in a wide mutual transatlantic flow. Since then West Germany has taken first place, reflecting extensive interchange with Austria, Switzerland, France and the UK, as well as its attraction for students from Scandinavia and the Mediterranean countries. In 1983-6 Germany was the most important European host country for students from the USA, Austria, Switzerland, France, Yugoslavia and Turkey; and the second host country for students from Spain, Greece, Belgium and Denmark. The USA and Germany, and after them France and Britain, were both the dominant home and host countries of student flows in the Atlantic world. A gradual shift in the transatlantic balance from inward flows to the US towards a greater focus within Western Europe, in the course of the 1980s, has been sharpened by the institutionalization of the EC's ERASMUS programme, which had grown from an initial 3,000 in 1987-8 to an estimated 25,000 in 1989-90: a classic example of a change in rules altering the direction of flows, with some 70% of the students from the EC Twelve coming to study in Britain, France or Germany.

Until the 1980s the countries of Eastern Europe were almost entirely excluded from this intensifying pattern of social interchange, which was pulling together the national societies of OECD Europe. Refugees flowed west, in substantial numbers from the GDR, small groups from elsewhere; and tourists flowed east. The political transformation of Europe at the end of the 1980s was foreshadowed by a gradual change in patterns of social interchange. Migration into West Germany – and Sweden – from Eastern Europe rose rapidly in the mid-1980s, as we have already noted. More significantly, tourist visits in both directions across the postwar European divide were rising, with an estimated 5m visits from the GDR to Federal Germany in 1988, and 4m visits from Hungary to Western Europe – the greater part to Austria. But few students or businessmen yet travelled with ease across central Europe; the formal and informal barriers, from visas to currency to bureaucratic controls, remained significant.

Can one also speak of a political core and periphery in contemporary Europe? Karl Deutsch saw political integration as 'a nuclear process', attracting a widening area around an initial core. Historical comparisons, he suggested, indicated that 'larger, stronger, more politically, administratively, economically and educationally advanced political units were found to form the cores of strength around which in most cases the integrative process developed.'[37] Monnet and his collaborators, as we have noted, held to a similar concept: the political dynamism displayed by their core group, the rules and institutions they established, serving to pull hesitant neighbours in. The initial group of political leaders who pushed forward the project of formal political integration all came from the region which stretched from the Low Countries to northern Italy, and which included the Rhineland and northern France. From the European Coal and Steel Community (ECSC) and WEU to the Schengen Agreement, the impetus for formal integration has come from within the same five to seven countries: most markedly from within the five countries which share the Rhine valley and its tributaries. The reasons for this are geographical and economic, as much as political. But the sense of political commitment, based upon the bitter experiences of shared history and the emergence of a community of shared assumptions and values, has been an essential factor in the creation of this core political community.

European values, European identity

'Europe' is a set of values as well as a collection of peoples and territories. Europe – or 'the West' – is identified both with a distinctive cultural tradition and with a set of political and cultural values which marks it out from other regions of the world. 'The European Community is one manifestation of that European identity', as Mrs Thatcher has noted; but European values and culture – this psychological community of shared assumptions and attitudes – spread a good deal further east and west.[38]

Here again the Atlantic and the European frameworks intertwine. The Atlantic Community was built upon defence of 'the West' against 'the East': of the 'Western values' of the rule of law, democratic government, and market economies, against the imperial autocracy represented by the Soviet Union to the east. It is in this sense that East European intellectuals insist on their affiliation to the West: as in Milan Kundera's definition of 'Mitteleuropa' as 'ein Stück des lateinischen Westens das unter russische Vorherrschaft geraten ist ... das geographisch im Zentrum, kulturell im Westen und politisch im Osten liegt.' Václav Havel, an intellectual become Czechoslovak President, referred in a speech to the Polish Parliament in January 1990 to the two countries' 'return to Europe': rejoining the West, after forty years of enforced exile from Western and European political society.[39]

The preamble to the Western European Union Treaty invokes the same symbolic values as the North Atlantic Treaty, to which it was deliberately subordinated. The preamble to the ECSC Treaty refers to 'the contribution which an organized and vital Europe can make', not to any independent or divergent enterprise. But it also refers, as has been noted, to the creation of 'a broader and deeper community among peoples long divided by bloody conflicts; ... to lay the foundation of a destiny henceforward shared.' A European community was to be *built*; not only through the dismantling of barriers to interchange among West European states, but also through the deliberate encouragement of new patterns of interaction – with the social learning which it was anticipated would grow out of familiar contacts – and through the creation of new institutions capable of generating political support and loyalty.

Nineteenth-century nation-states imposed common values, culture, historical identity, even language on their populations. The Atlantic Alliance and the economic organizations which accompanied it imposed a looser structure of rules about economic and political behaviour, enforced by the benevolent hegemony of the United States and by the acceptance of the other 'Atlantic states' of the legitimacy of American leadership. Within that wider context the European democracies insisted on a stricter set of rules about constitutional government and civil liberties. The Council of Europe, through its Consultative Assembly and its Commission and Court of Human Rights, symbolized this identification of Western Europe with the democratic values of individual freedom and limited government which intellectual historians traced from the Reformation, the eighteenth-century Enlightenment, and the French Revolution. Thus two member governments of NATO, Greece and Turkey, were suspended from participation in the

Council of Europe (but not from NATO or the OECD) when they came under military rule; and thus Hungary and Poland in 1989 saw closer association with the Council of Europe as symbolizing acceptance as 'Western' democracies.

Those who founded the European Community wanted, however, to go beyond this: to foster a more distinctive 'European identity', to replace the warring national identities which had brought the states of core Europe into repeated conflict. As the British, French, Italians and Germans had done in their deliberate nation-building efforts in the nineteenth century, the founders of the EC set out to create new myths and symbols to replace the old. Some of the sharpest disputes within the European Community have revolved around this aim. The embittered quarrel between Hallstein and de Gaulle about precisely how the Commission of the EEC should receive ambassadors, in 1964, reflected de Gaulle's determination to prevent the EEC developing the symbols of statehood – and Hallstein's intentions that it should acquire them. Repeated arguments about the status and powers of the European parliament, as an alternative focus of democratic legitimacy to established national parliaments, have derived their passion from similar attempts to undermine – or defend – the prior claims to loyalty and identity of the nation-state. Resistance to the EC Commission's attempts to establish its legal competence over the field of education, and above all opposition to the efforts (largely under the auspices of the Council of Europe) to create a more 'European history' to set the separate national histories within a common context, reflected the awareness of both proponents and opponents of the direct links between education, values, loyalty and legitimacy.[40]

The idea of a distinctive European identity, like the 'Atlantic idea' of the 1950s and 1960s, and the rediscovery of 'Mitteleuropa' in the 1980s, is an artificial construct: an attempt to rearrange tradition and history to suit current political needs, in which 'historiography threatens to become a political pamphlet' – as in the 'national' histories promoted 100 years ago.[41] The idea of a distinctive West European identity, Werner Weidenfeld has argued, was rooted in the postwar years 'in einer europäischen Anti-Nationalismus wie Anti-Communismus', and has grown progressively less distinct as those two initial thrusts have faded.[42] Why then has 'the evolution of a strong and coherent European identity' been welcomed in successive NATO communiqués, and contested in successive Atlantic crises over a 30-year period?[43]

The idea of an Atlantic community of shared values legitimized American leadership of its West European allies. The 'European idea', as Americans understood very well in the attempts to convert the Atlantic Alliance into a more equal partnership in the early 1960s, represented a claim to greater political autonomy, based upon the assertion of 'European' values and interests distinct from those which American leadership fostered.[44] The sensitivity of this assertion of a European political community which could not easily be subsumed within the American-led West was evident in the German, Dutch and British responses to de Gaulle's stark representation of the two alternatives; and evident also in the transatlantic crisis of 1973–4, during which the governments of the European Community solemnly negotiated and published a 'Declaration on European Identity'. The overwhelming importance of the Atlantic security guarantee made it necessary for European governments to deny what many knew to have been the case from the outset: that the attraction of the European idea contained threads of anti-Americanism as well as of anti-Communism, and that the idea of a 'third way' had much potential popular appeal.[45]

A Europe which defined itself separately from the East-West conflict, the ideal of some social democrats in the 1950s and increasingly of de Gaulle in the 1960s, undermined the entire postwar security structure. And yet the establishment of a more effective framework for decision-making within Western Europe *required* some sense of separate identity, some symbols of shared community to support the complex trade-offs and transfers which day-to-day cooperation involved. The greater the effectiveness of European cooperation, the more national politicians, officials, businessmen and opinion-leaders would look to that framework as a focus for common action when needed, rather than depending on the institutions of the Atlantic world. European cooperation diverted attention from Atlantic summitry to European Councils, from NATO political consultations to European political cooperation. It also diverted flows, not only of goods but also of people.

The argument during the 1980s over the EC's claims to competences in the educational and cultural spheres, over the appropriateness of measures to create a 'citizens' Europe', revolved around the competing priorities of national, European and Atlantic identity. The ERASMUS scheme, as we have noted above, has both increased the flow of students across Western Europe and to an extent diverted the flow from across the Atlantic to within the EC; just as the earlier bilateral programme of Franco-German exchanges, set up with the explicit intention of altering national attitudes and mental maps, at once increased the flow of young people between France and Germany and diverted it from other channels. The highly contested proposals for 'une Europe audio-visuelle', based upon the assumption that European culture – and the national cultures which it is seen as containing – are separate from and threatened by American mass culture, would similarly establish rules to alter the balance of cultural flows.

But alongside these examples of proactive formal integration, the evolution of social interaction and generational change has slowly and informally transformed the psychological map of Europe. The evidence, of opinion polls and elite surveys, is sparse and inadequate. But examination of survey data over the past 20 years indicates that the American 'ideological hegemony' which held the Atlantic system in place has slowly given way to a more European orientation.[46] The sense of a Soviet threat was part of the bedrock of Western Europe's Atlantic orientation; but the legitimacy of American alliance leadership rested on wider foundations. In the 1960s the majority of West Europeans saw America as 'more like us' than Eastern Europe and the USSR: its people more likeable, its leaders more trusted, its country and institutions more admired. During the 1970s this orientation weakened progressively, giving way to a perception of the two superpowers as equivalent, and of Europeans as belonging to a community of interests and values distinct from those of the United States: a shift which preceded by a considerable time the revival of formal integration within Western Europe, but which helped to lay the popular basis for it.[47] Political awareness of this shift, and of its potential implications for the Atlantic Alliance, explains the frequency of favourable references to a strengthening European identity '*within* the Alliance' in official declarations.[48]

Evidence of a set of European values distinct from those of the United States, including a stronger sense of social solidarity, equality, and the positive contribution of an active state, is sparser – and takes us close to the realm of political persuasion rather than of dispassionate analysis. Hartmut Kaelble's pioneering efforts suggest the gradual emergence of a distinctive European model of society: social-democratic, or social-capitalist, with developments in different national societies learning from one another.[49]

Values and attitudes are not static. They are shaped by experience and social learning, by mutual interactions over time, by the imagery and persuasiveness of intellectual and political leaders, and by shifts perceived in the external environment. The social integration of Western Europe has altered elite and popular assumptions about one another's national identities and about the space and the culture which they share.[50] The economic integration of Europe has made for a gradual homogenization of tastes and expectations. The integration of European communications has reshaped the messages the public receive and the areas over which they move. The emergence of a diffuse sense of European identity has *not* led to a transfer of loyalties from the national to the European level, as some of the early theorists and proponents of European integration foresaw. What we have observed across Western Europe over the last two decades is a shift towards multiple loyalties, with the single focus on the nation supplemented by European and regional affiliations above and below. Nor has it led to an exclusive identification of Europe with the formal European Community. *Eurobarometer* polls indicate that 'the most remarkable development between 1970 and 1986 is the increase in trust between France and Germany' – a tribute to the impact of deliberate policy and consistent political leadership. They also indicate that the most generally trusted and admired country among the publics of the EC member states was Switzerland, with Sweden also among the trusted smaller countries of the European space.[51]

'Modern man is not loyal to a monarch or a land or a faith, whatever he may say, but to a culture.'[52] Attempts to promote the idea of a distinctive European culture, tradition, or set of values, are thus of high political significance – whatever the apparent banality of arguments about European passports and postage stamps, frontier formalities, car number plates, 'Eurovision' programmes and youth exchanges.[53] The existence of shared European experiences and traditions for politicians to appeal to adds an additional dimension to the bargaining over rules and conflicting interests which constitutes the agenda of multilateral intergovernmental cooperation. Imprecise, in part invented, the claim to be part of a European community of shared culture and values has nevertheless become an important factor in European politics at the end of the 1980s. It has led the member governments of the European Community to recognize greater obligations to Hungary and Poland than they would admit to Bulgaria or Turkey, and has provided the political foundation for making the trade concessions and transfers of resources that they need, and also for setting the conditions which they must meet. 'The basis of our cooperation with the European Community', the EFTA heads of government declared in March 1989 in what could have served as a benchmark for the approaches of the East European countries, 'is a common cultural heritage, adherence to the fundamental values of democracy and human rights, geographical proximity and a high degree of interdependence in the fields of industry, trade and technological development'.[54] It is neither self-interest nor ideology alone, but the combination of these which makes for the emergence of a political community.

3
THE TRANSFORMATION OF WESTERN EUROPE

The formal integration of Western Europe began within a particular historical context. Reaction against the protectionist policies of the 1930s, revulsion against nationalism, dependence on American aid, and concern over the future of Germany combined to create the impetus for a tighter framework of rules to govern international relations among the reviving national governments of Western Europe. Much that obtained within that context has already passed into history. Developments in the 1980s have thrown more of its supporting assumptions, hopes and fears into question. Yet, after the apparent setbacks and disillusion which characterized West European integration in the late 1970s, the process of rule-building and institutional expansion has again been moving forward in recent years.

It would be naïve to imagine that the 12 current member governments of the European Community, after the initiation of the 1992 programme and the ratification of the Single European Act, are still pursuing entirely the same objectives as the six governments which signed the Treaties of Paris and Rome were persuaded to accept – let alone the several other governments which are hoping to join them during the 1990s. The pressures under which governments have operated in the 1980s, and the interests which they promote, have changed radically since the 1950s. How then are we to explain the persistence of formal West European political integration, and in particular the revived impetus which it has exhibited since the early 1980s? The idealist might argue the existence of an underlying commitment to European values, either among policy-making elites or among the mass public. The student of interdependence would point to the increase in economic and social flows across national boundaries, and to the mutual vulnerabilities and demands for shared management which they create. The institutionalist would answer in terms of the importance of structures and their effectiveness in shaping assumptions and outcomes. The economic determinist would underline the impact of economic and technical change, carrying governments and publics along in spite of their hesitations about the direction in which they are being taken. The international structuralist would look for hegemonic patterns of power, and for the place of West European integration in such patterns. The empiricist would deny the likelihood of any single dominant influence on such an untidy and intermittent process; but would find himself or herself nevertheless weaving together a framework of causation in order to reduce the messy realities of European politics to some coherent order. We are all forced to make assumptions about trends and their causation. Those who believe they are most free of theoretical presuppositions are, as Keynes remarked, the most contented slaves of outdated ideas.

The aim of this chapter is briefly to underline the transformation of Western Europe over the past 40 years, within the stable framework of rules and institutions which emerged after the end of the war. The shape of Western Europe was imposed upon it by the events of 1945–50: a core of allied countries, recognizing their ultimate dependence on each other and on the fate of the Western zones of Germany; an outer group of more reluctant allies; and a periphery of neutrals, sharply cut off by the 'iron curtain' from their prewar interchange with the countries to their east. That politically imposed geography has remained in place, but with increasingly significant modifications. The core of six politically integrated countries has expanded to twelve. The periphery has also expanded, as Finland's economic links have shifted from east to west and the Mediterranean countries have become increasingly dependent on their neighbours to the north. Most significantly of all, the countries of central Europe which were shut out behind the iron curtain have begun to rebuild old links, drawn towards Western Europe by powerful economic and political attraction.

Not all revolutions are visible and immediate. Some creep up on us, the magnitude of the changes involved being obscured by their gradual encroachment. World War II imposed violent and abrupt changes on the structure and boundaries of Europe, with immediate implications for patterns of economic relations and social interaction. It introduced American culture, American approaches to economics, business, and industrial production, American political ideas and influence on a much more extensive scale than Western Europe had known in the 1930s. Postwar governments, inspired by plans drawn up during the years of exile or imprisonment, were committed to bringing in new approaches to economic management and social welfare. But the brave new world which they set out to build was designed within the context of the society, economy and technology with which they were familiar, learning from the successes and failures they recalled from the prewar years. It was the ideas and assumptions which they had accumulated from these experiences that governed the reconstruction of Western Europe, within an Atlantic frame.

The world we have lost
The first tasks facing governments at the war's end were to feed and house their people, to cope with the flood of displaced persons – both their own citizens and refugees from other countries – and to begin to rebuild their shattered economies. The shape of those economies, it was assumed, would be not dissimilar to that of the 1930s: agriculture still a major sector and employer; heavy industry – coal, iron and steel, heavy engineering – the 'strategic' sector; automobiles and light engineering the rising industries. The impact on the civilian economy of the technological advances which wartime necessities had pressed forward was not immediately apparent. Governments (and demobilized pilots) saw the immense postwar potential of air transport and the value of supporting the manufacture of aircraft and aero-engines in peacetime. The role of scientific advance and technological applications in war had created a new 'strategic' sector for governments to foster and companies to move into. But these were investments for the future. The present requirements were to rebuild economies around the twin pillars of agriculture and industry.

In 1949–50, 29% of the French labour force were engaged in agriculture, 44% of the Italian. Ireland and Spain, economically much less developed, had over half of their labour forces in the primary sector. The Benelux countries and Denmark had a much higher percentage of their workforce in industry, as did Britain; though a quarter of Denmark's GDP came from the agricultural sector. The Western zones of Germany had lost their agricultural hinterland to the north-east; but the continued dependence on family farms and smallholdings in southern Germany left 24% of its workforce in agriculture. The 'tertiary' service sector was very much the *third* in importance after agriculture and industry, in every West European country. Coal, steel, electricity, railways, ships and ship-building were seen as the key to economic recovery, as they had been crucial to the capacity to rearm ten years before, and to the arms race which had preceded World War I. The Schuman Plan, imaginative and farsighted, proposed to integrate the economy and the political future of West Germany with its neighbours by locking its coal and steel industries – the key heavy industries – into a common framework.

The European economies accounted for one-third of world primary production in 1935–8, and nearly half of world industrial production. They emerged from World War II with their export industries destroyed, their markets uncertain, and a significant proportion of their overseas investments confiscated or sold off to finance their war efforts. The United States, the 'arsenal of democracy' during the war, its industries undisturbed by invasion or aerial bombing, dominated the postwar economy. In 1948 the USA alone accounted for over one-third of the world's GNP. It supplied half the world's exports of grain. It produced well over half the world's crude oil, and was thus the dominant force in world oil markets. For European countries, desperate to import machinery and raw materials, shortage of foreign exchange – which meant shortage of dollars, the world's dominant currency – was an acute constraint. The Marshall Plan thus speeded up the whole process of West European recovery, providing the finance to buy the materials and equipment to rebuild an industrial economy. It was also the clearest demonstration of the dominant position of the United States in the international economy, and of the enlightened self-interest with which American policy-makers exploited that position.

The security and stability which Western Europe has now enjoyed throughout the lifetimes of the majority of its inhabitants have obscured the intense insecurity which its inhabitants felt in the early postwar years. Economic deprivation was compounded by renewed internal and external threats, before the wartime allies had agreed any firm postwar settlement. Those who designed the institutions which manage Western Europe today were struggling to provide enough coal to keep the power stations going in the bitter winter of 1946–7, to supply the Western zones of Germany with the food which the Soviet zone would not supply, and to keep mines and transport going in the face of communist trade union activity. The extension of 'Western' protection and patronage to Greece and Turkey, through the enunciation of the 'Truman Doctrine' in March 1947, was a response under crisis conditions to a démarche from a British government struggling against power cuts, a frozen rail network, and the failure of its winter wheat crop. Jean Monnet was in Washington in April 1948, unsuccessfully attempting to persuade the US administration to increase the French bread ration from 200 to 250 grammes a day, using the threat to his government of the rhetoric of the CGT (the communist-led French trade union federation) to support his case.[1]

The Soviet threat as it appeared to West European eyes in the postwar years took several forms. There was the early refusal of the Soviet authorities to cooperate in the postwar administration of Germany, taking machinery, raw materials and food out of the country at one end as those responsible for the Western zones brought food and fuel in at the other. There was the imposition of Stalinist regimes on the countries occupied by Soviet forces, with initial communist-led coalitions giving way to total Communist Party control, rapidly in some countries, gradually in others. There was the domestic threat of subversion to economic recovery and political stability, of communist parties and communist trade unions apparently following instructions from Moscow. And there was the looming presence of the Red Army, still in place and in strength in the countries it occupied as the Western allies demobilized.[2]

The now-familiar boundaries between Western and Eastern Europe solidified only slowly. In 1946 the second largest Communist Party (after that of the Soviet Union) was in Italy, with over two million members; the third largest was in France, where in the elections of October 1945 the communists had emerged with the largest popular vote. Both countries included communist ministers in coalition governments; in France the defence ministry was allocated to them. Coalition governments in Finland and Czechoslovakia included communist ministers of the interior.

Vienna, as well as Berlin, was partly under Soviet occupation; Winston Churchill in his Fulton speech included Vienna among the list of historic European cities now behind the iron curtain. Yugoslavia differed little from Albania in its communist-led government.

In 1947–8 subversion seemed the clearest and most imminent danger. The Berlin blockade represented a more direct military threat, with American atomic weapons being moved to air bases in Britain to deter conventional attack. The North Korean invasion of its southern neighbour, in June 1950, following Soviet testing of its own atomic weapons, completed the crystallization of the dominant perception into a direct military Soviet threat, whereby the Red Army was seen as a positive danger to the Western zones of Germany, and therefore to Western Europe as a whole.

For, out of this confusion of postwar anxieties and crises, it was the future of Germany which was of necessity the central concern of every other European government, north and south, east and west. In 1939 the British and French governments had gone to war with Germany over Poland, to which they felt a continuing postwar obligation. The symbolic importance of Czech democracy and independence owed much to memories of Munich. Postwar developments in Poland and Czechoslovakia thus carried particular political significance for Western governments and publics. But the future of Germany was the central issue of national security for *all* those countries occupied or attacked over the previous six years. The failure of the wartime allies to agree on the postwar constitution or boundaries of Germany set the framework for the disputes within the Allied Kommandatura, for rising mutual suspicion over one another's intentions, and for the Western currency reform and the Berlin blockade and airlift which followed. It was clear to all concerned that control over a reviving Germany, with its 63 million inhabitants (45 million in the Western zones, and 18 million in the East) would mean for either of the emerging camps control over the whole of central Europe, and that a revived and independent Germany would raise once more the whole question of European hegemony or European balance. The Anglo-French treaty of alliance which was signed at Dunkirk in March 1947 was explicitly directed against the threat 'that Germany should again become a danger to peace'. The five-nation Treaty of Western European Union signed in Brussels a year later was designed to guard against the emerging Soviet threat; but its signatories put on record their determination 'to take any and all steps which might become necessary should there be a return to a German policy of aggression.'

The Atlantic Alliance which followed in 1949 was aimed at the emerging Soviet military threat. But it took not only the shock of apparent Soviet military expansion in Korea but also intense American pressure to persuade Germany's Western neighbours to consider accepting the German contribution to the conventional defence of Western Europe which American strategists thought essential to contain the Soviet army. Political integration under such circumstances seemed to its proponents in France and the Low Countries to be less an ideal than a painful necessity, reconciling conflicting pressures through an imaginative leap. The French National Assembly nevertheless refused to make that leap when the completed European Defence Community Treaty was presented for ratification in 1953. American threats to reappraise their commitment to Western Europe gained instead a revision of the Brussels Treaty, extended to include Italy and Germany, and hedged about with safeguards over German military forces and their equipment.

Britain and France, of course, were still substantial imperial powers, their hesitancy over any irrevocable commitment to a more politically integrated Western Europe partly reflecting their continuing extra-European ambitions – and their need to maintain national armed forces to protect those ambitions. The Dutch attempt to regain their East Indian empire, after the end of the Japanese occupation, rapidly foundered on Indonesian insurgency, American disapproval of 'colonialism', and domestic economic constraints. The French reoccupation of Indo-China met with similar American criticism, until first the collapse of Kuomintang China and then the Korean war transformed the American perspective. Later French governments attempted similarly to persuade their American patron that the rebellion which broke out in Algeria in 1955 should be seen as a battle against communism rather than a colonial war – but without success. The British were more successful: in defeating the communist forces in Greece and in persuading the Americans to take over the ensuing commitment; in defeating the Malayan insurrection which grew out of the wartime resistance to the Japanese, and in presenting it to the Americans as a defeat for communist expansion.

41

West European economic and military dependence on the United States made American approval and patronage essential to success at home and abroad. Between 1947 and 1951 American assistance under the Marshall Plan amounted to nearly $12 billion, accounting in 1948-9 for 5% of Italian national income, 6.5% of French, 11% of Dutch.[3] European rearmament in the wake of the Korean war similarly depended on American subsidy. Between 1953 and 1958, under the Mutual Security Act, the US offshore procurement programme transferred $3.3 billion to European defence spending, along with substantial transfers of technology for weapons systems built under licence. The USA, the USSR and Germany thus provided the three interlinked and dominating reference points for the foreign policies of other West European governments, for over a decade after World War II: the United States as the essential provider and hegemon, the Soviet Union as the dominant threat, and Germany as the underlying problem.

Western Europe revived

Economic 'recovery' – the rebuilding of the economies of West European countries devastated by the war – proceeded through the 1950s. The European Recovery Program which had administered Marshall Plan aid had been wound up in 1952, its coordinating functions taken over by the OEEC. Military assistance, which peaked in 1952-3, gradually ran down until its end in 1959. The European Payments Union, set up under American sponsorship in 1950 to ease intra-European transactions under conditions of international dollar shortage, was wound up in 1958. That year might indeed be taken as the one in which Western Europe ceased to be ancillary to the American economy and became again a self-sustaining competitor. The US balance of trade deteriorated sharply that year, with flows of foreign aid and investment converting a small trade surplus into a balance-of-payments deficit. Trade balances in Europe were rising – particularly that of Federal Germany, which was accumulating gold and currency reserves as those of the USA began to decline.

The years between 1958 and 1968 can be seen, in retrospect, as the Indian summer of European centrality in the international system. A truncated Europe, cut off from its traditional markets and partners to the east, had nevertheless become a prosperous counterpart to the

United States, within an 'Atlantic Community' which in 1960 accounted for 58% of world trade and over two-thirds of global GNP. American investment was flowing strongly into Europe, bringing managerial and technical innovation with it. European agriculture, like American, was witnessing a rapid and sustained increase in productivity – the basis for heated transatlantic disputes from the mid-1960s on. The total GNP of the EC Six amounted to 37% of the American in 1960, to 42% in 1965. The figures for OEEC Europe – which became OECD Europe with the reform of that organization in 1960–61 – were 71% and 74% respectively.

Europe also remained unquestionably the central focus of the global security system. The Korean war had been interpreted as an indication of a clear Soviet military threat to Western Europe, sparking off the transformation of the loose Atlantic Alliance into NATO and the ambitious rearmament programme which followed. The series of crises over Berlin between 1958 and 1961 brought American reinforcements to Europe, instead of the gradual withdrawals which Washington had hoped that the build-up of West German military forces would allow. US conventional forces rose to 440,000 in 1962, after the reductions of the previous three years: overwhelmingly the most important US land and air commitment outside the continental United States. In August 1961 Soviet and American tanks faced each other at close range across the zonal boundaries of Berlin. What was to the Soviet Union a matter of stemming the haemorrhage of emigrants from East Germany, with its threat to the stability of the entire Soviet position in central Europe, appeared to Western governments and publics as clear evidence of the stark military confrontation between East and West and of its focal point in the struggle over Germany.

These were also the years in which European countries completed their disengagement from empire – sometimes tragically, sometimes successfully. The precipitate Belgian withdrawal from the Congo drew the United States into confrontation in southern Africa for the first time, as cold war politics replaced colonial rule. The Algerian rebellion brought down the French Fourth Republic, though President de Gaulle rescued French prestige and economic interests by converting the remainder of France's African possessions into a 'Community' of states under French patronage. British decolonization in Africa, which began with the independence of Ghana in 1957 and was completed – except for the unhappy case of Rhodesia – with the independence of Tanzania in 1964, left the United Kingdom at the centre of a multi-racial Commonwealth which still looked to London for trade, investment, and if necessary military support. The transition from empire was seen as diffusing European influence, not displacing it; American initiatives on multilateral programmes for international development were welcome supports in resisting the Marxist temptations of anti-colonialism, rather than being threats to established positions and markets. Britain and France retained significant military forces and commitments outside Europe, as well as investments, trading and cultural links. It was the United States which successfully pressed for Japan to be accepted into the OECD on its formation, against the opposition of West European governments which saw only a protectionist developing country with the potential to disrupt their Asian markets.

Britain and France failed to stem the rise of Arab nationalism in decolonized North Africa and the Middle East, a region of informal European empire between and after the wars: most signally in their joint intervention on the Suez Canal in 1956. Iraq followed Syria and Egypt from the 'Western' to the 'radical' camp in 1958, after a coup deposed its monarchy. The French withdrawal from Algeria in 1962 marked the end of the imperial myth of France on both shores of the Mediterranean. The newly independent Tunisian government had supported the Algerian NLF. The Libyan monarchy was overthrown by a group of army officers in 1969, threatening the future of British and American bases in the country. Britain's gradual military withdrawal from the Mediterranean, marked most definitively by the disappearance of the Mediterranean fleet it had maintained since the eighteenth century, together with the reduction in France's political and military position, left the United States Sixth Fleet as the dominant force maintaining order on Western Europe's southern flank.

American power and patronage, supported by the modest British forces still stationed in the Persian Gulf, also continued to maintain a considerable degree of stability in the Middle East: most crucially in Iran, Saudi Arabia, Kuwait and the strategically vital states of the Gulf. Oil from the Middle East, supplied in increasing quantities at prices which were falling in real terms, with new discoveries adding to the downward pressure on prices and increasing European confidence in future supply, was the driving force behind the long Western economic boom of the 1960s. The oil flowed from the wells to Western Europe under the control of a small group of companies, predominantly American, but also British, French and Dutch, operating as an informal cartel, under the protection and leadership of American policy. Only the aggressive efforts of Mattei's ENI (Ente Nazionale Idrocarburi) in North Africa threatened to disturb this managed market.

Economic recovery was sustained into continuing growth also through transatlantic cooperation, Keynesian demand management, and the confidence given to business throughout the Atlantic world by the reduction of trade barriers within Western Europe and within GATT. Meanwhile, the balance of political and economic weight within Western Europe was changing subtly. Great Britain's economy, the least physically damaged by the war and the greatest beneficiary of Marshall aid, was the largest in Western Europe throughout the early postwar years. The reviving West German economy overtook it in 1961, overcoming the loss of territory and of the industrial regions around Berlin and in Silesia, to reclaim the position it had captured at the end of the nineteenth century. The French economy, guided by successive indicative plans and by extensive government intervention, surpassed the British in 1966. The pound sterling, which together with the dollar had formed the basis of the international reserve system since the Bretton Woods agreements, was devalued in 1967, after a series of sterling crises. In contrast the French government, which had successfully maintained a stable franc since 1958, was accumulating gold reserves and explicitly challenging the ability of the USA to finance its deepening deficits through the dollar's reserve role. The Italian economy was still heavily dependent on agriculture, with an acute contrast between the dynamism of its industrial north and the poverty of the Mezzogiorno. Spain remained outside most European economic and political developments, with only the beginnings of industrial modernization penetrating its protected economy.

Key issues of industrial modernization, as they appeared to French technocrats, British planners, and German bankers in the late 1950s, included automobile production, aircraft and aero-engines, telecommunications and atomic energy – this last a military secret until mid-1945, its civil potential as a source of power being a priority in British and French research and development programmes in the 1950s. There were those among the negotiators at Messina, before the size and exploitability of Middle East oil had become apparent, who saw the creation of a European Atomic Energy Community as more crucial to West European interests, economic and military, than the proposed common market – with the aims of providing the cheap energy needed to fuel continuing economic growth, giving European suppliers a technological edge in world markets, and replacing Europe's dependence on limited and depleted supplies of coal.[4] These were the years which saw major advances in the electrification of Western Europe's railways, and the phasing out of steam; which witnessed major programmes of port modernization, as seaborne trade expanded; which saw competitive plans to modernize and increase national steel production, still one of the accepted primary indicators of industrial strength. National motorway networks were beginning to be built, following the German and American models. National telephone networks were being automated and extended, and international links improved: the first European direct dialling link opened between London and Paris in 1963. Television transmission was also spreading, as national authorities authorized second channels to diversify programmes.

These were also the years of emerging West European fears of the 'American challenge': both of the increasing power of American business, operating through multinational companies with the weight of the US domestic market behind them and on occasion the support of the US government, and of the 'technology gap' represented – most visibly – by American air and space programmes and their associated innovations in electronics and materials. The scale of public investment which seemed necessary in research and development led the British and French governments, Europe's technological leaders, both into bilateral programmes of cooperation – first Concorde, then proposals for military aircraft and helicopters – and into multilateral consortia, of which the European Launcher Development Organization and the European Space Research Organization were the first.

Both governments, as they adjusted their military and civil technological ambitions to the constraints of their national budgets, began to look increasingly towards West Germany as a preferred partner. They saw there an economy with substantial public and private capital to invest, and without as yet the competing design teams and commercial ambitions which bedevilled cooperation between Britain and France. The revival of the French economy had contributed to the intense sense of rivalry between Britain and France in Western Europe in the 1960s, as Europe's two nuclear powers, with continuing global responsibilities. Germany's revived economic weight entered into the balance only indirectly, while political leaders there were still too conscious of the immense restrictions which World War II had imposed upon them, as well as of their country's immediate dependence on continuing American protection for security from the Soviet threat, to wish to take on any explicit leadership role in Western Europe.

The world we have found

The ten fat years which Western Europe experienced between 1958 and 1968 were followed by ten very thin years, in which economic growth faltered and the centrality of Europe in the international economy and in the international security system was repeatedly challenged. American intervention in Vietnam brought, from 1965 on, a decline in the number and quality of US forces in Europe, a rapid deterioration in the US balance of payments, and increasing pressure on the European allies to support both the dollar and the US military commitment. There followed the 'shocks' of 1971–4: the suspension of dollar convertibility and the subsequent breakdown of the Bretton Woods system, accompanied by a downturn in the growth of international trade and GNP; the loss of control over Middle East oil supplies, the 1973 Middle East war, the embargo and the quadrupling of oil prices which followed. West European governments, like their counterparts in Washington and Tokyo, struggled to adjust to altered and adverse international circumstances, to changing patterns of American policy, and to the changing balance of economic – but not yet political or military – weight between the United States, Western Europe and Japan.

Western Europe emerged into the 1980s with an economy and society substantially altered from those of the boom years of the 1960s. One of its most striking – and under-recognized – transformations was in the productivity of its agriculture. The guaranteed prices of the 1960s regime had sparked off a rise in production which was extended by technical advances, in mechanization, in fertilizers and pesticides, and in plant breeding, which made Western Europe America's main competitor in global export markets. While through the 1970s agricultural production in Eastern Europe and the Soviet Union stagnated, the total grain crop of the EC Twelve rose steadily. Milk production grew even more rapidly, and there were similar increases in beef production. Yet by 1980 only 9.5% of the workforce of the EC Twelve was employed in agriculture, compared with 37% in industry and 53.5% in the rapidly diversifying service sector.

West European industry had fared far less well under the impact of sharper international competition, slower domestic and international economic growth, and continuing technical change. 'Industrial adjustment' was both a national and a regional preoccupation during the 1970s, as Japan (and behind it the newly industrializing countries of East Asia) captured European export markets in Africa, Asia and North America, and began to secure an increasing share of the market in some industrial sectors within Western Europe itself. Surplus capacity in steel, textiles, and chemicals led to complex negotiations on subsidies and closures, with the United States protesting about distortions to international trade, and the trade unions protesting about losses of jobs. Rates of unemployment rose sharply, from an average of 2.5% in the EC Twelve in 1973 to an average of 7.3% in 1979; in spite of some improvement thereafter, European unemployment rates remained stubbornly above American rates throughout the 1980s. The apparatus of the welfare state which economic growth and rising tax revenues had funded was becoming, it appeared, a hindrance to the shifts of policy and investment needed in harder circumstances. 'Eurosclerosis' was a term as current inside Western Europe as outside. Rising unemployment meant rising expenditure on social security, while at the same time the changing age structure of Western Europe's population was increasing state spending on pensions and health care. Employment laws and trade union strength made the reduction in real wages needed to adjust to the rise in imported energy costs difficult to achieve without inflation; in almost all West European countries inflation therefore rose rapidly during the second half of the 1970s, and was brought under control only with difficulty in the years which followed.

Equally worrying was the apparent decline in Western Europe's underlying competitive advantage, as Japan caught up with America in technical innovation, leaving behind the government-supported national champions of European enterprise. European inability to compete seemed most marked in the new technologies, where in semiconductors and in consumer electronics Japanese companies rapidly established a dominant position. This in turn sparked off a series of alliances and mergers, and of demands for political responses in various forms – which we will explore further in the following chapters.

Yet the European economy of the 1980s was – unemployment apart – *not* a picture of stagnation and decline. The greater weight of social expenditure and the entrenched position of economic interests had made for a slower, more painful and in most countries more inflationary response to the shocks of the early 1970s than that offered in the United States or – most of all – in Japan. But by the early 1980s some substantial adjustments had taken place. The average rate of growth for the EC Twelve between 1978 and 1988 was 2.1%, compared with 2.9% for the USA and 4.3% for Japan; though in the five years 1983–8 the gap had narrowed marginally to 2.5% as against 4.2% and 4.6%. Each year the gap between West European growth and East European stagnation was becoming more stark. The rising flow of Japanese investment into Western Europe was dwarfed by the flood of intra-European investment and of European investment in the United States.[5] European OECD still accounted for 44% of total OECD output and 44% of world trade in 1984, compared with the United States' 35% and 13%, in spite of the relative rise of the East Asian economies in world production and trade.[6]

The West European economy itself was becoming each year less and less an interdependent group of national economies, and more and more an integrated regional economy. The ratio of trade to GDP within all West European countries was rising steadily; the proportion of that trade accounted for by interactions with other West European countries varied from 55% to 80%. After a period in the late 1970s when the intensification of intra-European trade appeared to be faltering, economic integration continued to progress. This integration was of an increasingly different character from that of the 1960s. Europe-wide companies were now much more common, in manufacturing, retailing, and – in spite of the remaining national regulatory obstacles – in finance and transport: buying in components from several countries for final assembly in one, two or more countries, to be marketed by continent-wide campaigns often through multinational retail chains.[7] In the 1960s the most effectively multinational companies in European markets had, with only a handful of exceptions, been American-owned; in the 1980s they were also Dutch, Swiss, Swedish, British, Italian, French and German, as well as a rising number of Japanese.

The interdependent European international economy of the early 1960s had two focal points, in Britain and Germany. With the relative decline of the British economy throughout the 1960s and 1970s, the integrated European economy of the 1980s had one incontestable core. The German economy accounted for 26% of the total GDP of the EC Twelve in 1985. It was the major trading partner of virtually every other European member of OECD; with all except the Netherlands, Ireland and Norway it was running a consistent trading surplus. The D-mark had become Europe's key currency, the core of the European Monetary System and the main reference point for Austrian, Swedish and Swiss central bankers. London had retained its position as Europe's most important international financial market; but it was Frankfurt which counted most with New York and Tokyo in the management of the world's currencies.

The French economy, Western Europe's second largest, was not only intensively integrated with its German neighbour but deeply dependent upon it. The failure of the Mitterrand administration's 'dash for growth' in 1981–3 had left a deep impression not only in France but in several of Germany's other partners of their vulnerability to divergent German policies, and of the absolute necessity of closer economic cooperation in such circumstances. The continued dynamism of north Italian industry had carried Italy's GDP to rival Britain's for third place – exact rankings depending on inexact statistics. The Spanish economy was emerging as an important industrial producer, aided by investment from Germany, France, Italy and Japan. Sweden and Switzerland, very closely linked to the German economy, were also through their multinational companies major players Europe-wide.

Social interaction across Western Europe had witnessed an even more remarkable transformation, as was noted in Chapter 2. The 1960s had seen a flow of migrant labour northwards from Italy, Greece, Spain, Portugal and Yugoslavia, and a compensating flow of tourists southwards to the Mediterranean. The 1980s saw *far* larger flows of tourists, and students, moving across frontiers throughout OECD Europe. Patterns of migrant labour had become more complex: as Italians and Greeks returned home to their more prosperous economies; as Poles, Turks and North Africans moved into Western Europe's most prosperous areas to replace them; and as cross-border employment became more common, in Brussels, London, Amsterdam, Paris, Frankfurt, and other major European cities.

The integration of European markets had made for a certain homogenization of tastes and fashions, as British and Italian knitwear, Danish lager, French cheese and German executive cars carried the same cachet throughout Europe, promoted by the same advertising campaigns. Television was exerting an identical homogenizing influence: available on cable in cities such as Brussels and Amsterdam on over a dozen channels in up to four languages, with national networks pursuing joint productions and buying in one another's programmes – as well as a large proportion of American programmes – to fill their screens without breaking their budgets. While the popular printed media remained entirely national, Europe's business and political elites were increasingly scanning the same selection of international journals and newspapers, available on newsstands throughout the continent.

Western Europe's underlying security situation had also shifted progressively since the late 1960s. Out of the transatlantic disagreements on East-West relations, from the mid-1970s on, had emerged an underlying consensus that West European perceptions of the Soviet threat and of the potential benefits of closer political and economic relations between the two halves of Europe differed substantially from those of the United States – and that American policy-makers no longer saw central Europe as the main focus of their global security concerns. Well before the appointment of Mikhail Gorbachev as First Secretary, the evident weakness of the economies of the socialist countries had been brought home by the crisis in Poland in 1980–81, by the inability of East European countries to repay their debts, and by the efforts of the Hungarians to develop closer links with their Western neighbours as a way out of their own structural economic difficulties. West European tourists had been spreading out across Eastern Europe since the 1960s; Eastern Europeans had been struggling to gain access to Western Europe, for education and advancement as much as for political reasons.

If the 1960s appeared to have re-established Western Europe's central international position, as partner to the USA within an

Atlantic world, the 1980s must be seen much more as a period of multipolarity and regionalism, in which West European countries formed only one grouping among a number of global players. In 1960 31% of the United States' external trade had been with Western Europe, its most important regional trading partner. Twenty years later, Japan had long since overtaken Germany as America's most important trading partner, and US transpacific trade comfortably exceeded transatlantic trade. Japan's importance to the United States was far wider than this: as investor in US government and private securities, as technological competitor, as key partner in Asia. The United States still retained its military commitments in central and southern Europe, though its policy-makers saw them more as a part of America's global commitment to the maintenance of international order – in, for example, the Middle East – rather than as a commitment to Europe alone. Alongside Japan, Federal Germany counted, for political and economic reasons, as the United States' most important partner: an uncomfortable reality which the presence of Britain, France and Italy at the annual 'Group of Seven' summits helped to veil.

A continent transformed

Political integration does not take place in a vacuum. The context is set by international and domestic trends, by the prevailing balance of power, by economic and technical stability or change. The aim of formal integration measures is to reshape and redirect patterns of economic and social interaction, by altering the rules which govern their flow. This chapter has deliberately played down the importance of such political rule-making, in order to give more emphasis to informal developments and underlying trends. The chapters which follow set out to redress the balance by considering the interplay between formal international political structures and the informal processes of international integration.

4

THE DYNAMICS OF INTEGRATION

Modernization and integration go together. Subsistence economies revolve around the village and the tribe. What little communication they maintain with outsiders is limited to intermittent trade and occasional raids; what sense of community within a wider society there may be is dependent upon religion, myth and ceremony. The growth of trade and of towns, the improvement of transport and the spread of education created the basis for larger political units held together by more than military force, capable of outlasting the supremacy of successive conquerors. Industrialization, the steam engine and the railway, the shift of population from farms to factories and from villages to cities, provided the basis both for popular nationalism and for centralized states.

Economic development, technical change and their accompanying social patterns have thus provided the underlying impetus for the historical processes of integration, moving from small communities to nations and on towards intensive international interaction, and from local law and loyalties to state sovereignty and on to multilateral management. But this has not been a continuous or even movement. Political intervention has often interrupted the flow, and has repeatedly attempted to shape and reshape it into different patterns.

'Integration' is as imprecise a term as 'independence', 'authority', 'sovereignty', or 'state'; and as widely used – and misused – by politicians and political scientists, economists, sociologists and lawyers. Each of these professional groups focuses its arguments round different aspects of the phenomenon. Few except such historicists as Hegel and Marx have claimed to encompass the full complexity of social, economic and political integration within a single theory. All attempts at a systematic overview of long-term developments risk degenerating into scientism – giving a pretended theoretical coherence to the author's underlying preferences. The aim here is to explore the range of approaches, explicit and implicit, which are useful in understanding recent West European trends. It is not assumed that any one 'key' factor is to be found among the various forces which have pushed Western Europe together: neither political, economic nor social developments are amenable to unicausal explanations.

Given the diversity of definitions of integration, some working distinctions are necessary. Two overlapping lines of differentiation are drawn throughout the remainder of this volume: between *formal integration* and *informal integration*, and between *political integration* and *economic and social integration*. Formal integration consists of deliberate actions by authoritative policy-makers to create and adjust rules, to establish common institutions and to work with and through those institutions; to regulate, channel, redirect, encourage or inhibit social and economic flows, as well as to pursue common policies. Informal integration consists of those intense patterns of interaction which develop without the intervention of deliberate governmental decisions, following the dynamics of markets, technology, communications networks and social exchange, or the influence of religious, social or political movements. Informal integration is thus a matter of flows and exchanges, of the gradual growth of networks of interaction. By definition it is a continuous process in which sharp discontinuities are rare. Disintegration is of course represented by the decline of such flows and exchanges; integration is in no sense an inexorable or unidirectional process. Formal integration is by definition a discontinuous process, proceeding treaty by treaty, regulation by regulation, decision by decision.

A further distinction is drawn between *proactive* and *responsive* formal integration. Proactive formal integration has a deliberate and explicit political aim: to redirect informal flows into patterns other than those which market forces or social trends might independently have created. Nation-building is the classic example of proactive formal integration: removing some barriers and raising others, marking out clear boundaries, encouraging particular patterns of interaction and discouraging – even forbidding – others. Responsive formal integration is more characteristic of *laissez-faire* government and of much detailed intergovernmental cooperation: reacting to economic and social changes by adjusting rules and regulations as far as seems necessary and proves acceptable.

Political integration is a matter of identity and loyalty: of the emergence of a political community based upon shared values and mutual trust out of previously separate and mistrustful groups.[1] Social integration is a measure of the intensity of non-violent human interaction, whether among groups which retain a sense of separate identity or among communities in the process of political integration. Economic integration is a measure of the intensity of economic transactions: of the growth of an interdependent economy out of previously autonomous economic units.

These are of course 'ideal type' concepts, abstracted from the messy complexities of historical experience. Economic exchange brings with it social contact. Political integration depends upon a degree of social interchange, and is difficult to develop or maintain without the perception of mutual economic benefits. But, again, there is no simple or inexorable transition from contact through trade to the emergence of political community. The development of a politically integrated British nation out of previously distinct national and regional communities in some respects preceded extensive social integration between England and Scotland, even between southern and northern England.[2] Extensive social interchange between the different states of the eighteenth-century Holy Roman empire preceded the growth of a widespread sense of common membership of a German nation, with the progressive transfer of loyalty and identity to this wider community.

Formal integration and political integration overlap extensively; but they are not identical. In the optimistic years after the formation of the European Economic Community there were some who believed that political integration would develop across Western Europe without the assistance of further formal measures, beyond the initial institutionalization of the Communities themselves. Experience of working together, the learning process which comes from successful collaboration, would lead national officials, business and interest group representatives – under the guidance of the Commission – to 'upgrade the common interest', and so progressively to transfer their loyalties from their national level to a wider European community.[3] Others looked to political parties to provide the social learning which would widen horizons and build mutual trust, interacting through the international groupings of socialists, liberals and Christian democrats which emerged within Western Europe after World War II, with the additional stimulus provided by the Consultative Assembly of the Council of Europe and the various institutions of the European Community and Western European Union.[4]

The experience of the quarter century since then – to be discussed further below – has demonstrated that social learning is a much more complex process. There is no such straightforward transfer of loyalties from one dominant focus to another; obligations, identities, become diffused among different levels of community, rather than transformed, by continuing interaction. The single focus of loyalty which was the objective and the characteristic of the centralizing nation-state was imposed by formal and forceful measures; it did not evolve out of loosely-directed cooperation, economic interaction, and social interchange.

National integration: the interaction of formal and informal processes
National integration preceded international integration. The concept of international integration itself emerged only during the 1950s, in response to the developments described in Chapter 3. The nineteenth century witnessed in Europe 'a greater and more continuous increase in the integration of the political community and the power of the state than was achieved in all previous history'. The forces producing this 'centralization of the community and the associated rise of the centralizing state ... have in each case been those technical and economic changes which have steadily transformed the quality of political and social existence since the beginning of the 19th century and continue to transform it'.[5] Formal political integration was made possible by informal changes in industrial production, in transportation and in social mobilization, leading to the urbanization of a population which had until then been scattered among thousands of small rural settlements. These changes brought the mass of people into contact with government for the first time.

There was no single pattern of development across Europe. In

Britain, the first country to experience industrialization and urbanization, the role of government was relatively limited. The attraction of London and of the English political and social elites was sufficiently strong for many in Scotland and Wales to assist in the assimilation of their own communities; the provision of private capital was sufficient to support the rapid spread of railways and the development of heavy industries. The French state played a consistently more active role, both in the social integration of regional minorities and in the promotion of transport links and industrial development. In Germany and in Italy a sense of nationhood existed – at least among intellectual and urban elites – before any centralized political institutions were created. The alliance between Prussia and German nationalists, after the failure of the 1848 Frankfurt 'parliament', helped to create an integrated Reich out of a patchwork of kingdoms and principalities; the support of Italian nationalists outside its territories, fighting on behalf of the idea of a united Italy, was crucial to the legitimization of the house of Savoy as national unifiers. Austria-Hungary, too diverse to impose a dominant culture and ideology on its score of overlapping ethnic groups, attempted to industrialize and modernize without promoting mass social integration, as a dual monarchy and a multilingual state. The upsurge of competing nationalisms which urbanization and education encouraged was contained until 1914; but the war which broke out over Serbian national ambitions ended in defeat and disintegration.

National integration was the child of the industrial revolution. The agricultural societies of eighteenth-century Europe supported a small but internationally integrated social and political elite. The intellectual impact of the Enlightenment reinforced the dominance of French language and culture, from Edinburgh to St Petersburg. Adam Smith regarded his visits to Voltaire as among the high points of his continental education.[6] The courts of Prussia and Russia corresponded with Voltaire. When Wellington and Blücher met, victorious, on the field of Waterloo, they greeted each other in French – the natural *lingua franca* of any educated gentleman under Europe's *ancien régime*. The first stirrings of nationalism among France's neighbours came often from among the growing bourgeoisie, reacting against the 'cosmopolitanism' of their aristocratic rulers.[7]

The explosion of French power and influence between 1789 and 1815 provoked a second wave of national self-consciousness, in

57

Spain, in Italy, and above all in Germany.[8] But these were largely movements of intellectuals, seeking where they could to win over the rising class of merchants and industrialists – from which most of the intellectuals were themselves drawn. Popular nationalism stemmed from the social mobilization brought about by the dual shift from villages to towns and cities and from small-scale enterprise to factories and large firms. It was strengthened by the national education which industrial society needed and state authority promoted. It accompanied the spread of industrial society from West to East across Europe, to provoke confusion and conflict among the intermingled languages and faiths of central and eastern Europe.[9]

European states had coped with a high degree of internal non-integration in the eighteenth century. French internal tolls were not abolished until the 1789 revolution; Prussia did not eliminate internal tariffs on trade until 1818, responding to pressure from commercial and industrial interests and to acceptance within the Prussian government that economic strength required an integrated economy.[10] Differences in local time within Britain were eroded in the 1830s and 1840s by the spread of railways, with their demand for uniform timetables, though it was not until 1880 that an Act of Parliament officially standardized Greenwich Mean Time throughout the British Isles.[11] Austria-Hungary allowed a diversity of rules of the road among its provinces until its demise; the new rump state of Austria inherited this diversity, attempting to impose a uniform 'keep to the right' rule under legislation passed in 1929 which was fully implemented only after the *Anschluss* of 1938.[12] Increasing informal, undirected economic and social interchange required the removal of old formal rules and regulations and the imposition of new, even in the most *laissez-faire* of states. More interventionist states, following the theories of Friedrich List rather than of Adam Smith, imposed new rules with the intention of encouraging economic development and promoting social unity.

'With a handful of exceptions, modern nations are an amalgam of historical communities which possessed a fairly clear sense of separate identity in the past but have been brought together by various economic, social and political developments. The process by which they are brought together is known as political integration.'[13] That process, however, included, in all successful attempts by centralizing governments to build nation-states out of diverse populations, a considerable degree of compulsion by already powerful arms of central authority: the suppression of minority languages, the imposition of national military service, the enforcement of tighter border controls, discrimination against aliens, and the use of war to extend national territory, national power and national pride. It also included official promotion of integrating national values, and of a 'national myth': through state education above all, but in most countries also through the 'national' churches and through a greater or lesser degree of official censorship of dissident views.

The nation-states of Western Europe had thus established their authority by the beginning of the twentieth century, retaining their basic unity through the traumas of the Great War of 1914–18, which destroyed the defeated empires of central and eastern Europe, and even through periods in which contending movements fought to control the instruments of legitimate national authority. World War II shook more profoundly the authority of those states which were occupied or defeated, and convinced many intellectuals within them that a new European order was needed to prevent another descent into national rivalry and war. But the arguments which they advanced in the 1940s had only limited appeal to politicians and economic planners, for whom the national economy was still the primary frame of reference, with the technologies needed to re-establish economic growth still apparently obtainable and affordable within the national context. Nor did they have much resonance for mass publics, which in spite of the immense upheavals of military service, prisoners of war, forced labour, deportation and refugees retained their national loyalties and mental maps – more strongly in those countries which had suffered less from the war, most strongly in those which had escaped direct involvement or occupation, most weakly in defeated Italy and in defeated and divided Germany.[14]

The nation-states of central and eastern Europe – those ill-defined and shifting terms of political geography – had established their boundaries and their authority only out of the 'creative destruction' of the Great War.[15] Experiencing later the dynamic and disruptive changes of industrialization and urbanization, more painfully aware of the costs and benefits of national integration and the problems of reconciling 'state' and 'nation' where ethnic communities overlap, several of the early students of the processes of modernization and international integration were, hardly surprisingly, marked by the collapse of Austria-Hungary. Karl Deutsch was the son of a German-speaking member of the Czech parliament. While a student at the German University in Prague, his opposition to *Grossdeutsch-land* sentiment led him to complete his doctorate at the Czech-speaking Charles University.[16] Karl Polanyi was a member of the Budapest Bar and a captain in the Austro-Hungarian army, then a journalist and lecturer in Vienna, before his exile in London and the United States.[17] Joseph Schumpeter, born in Moravia and educated in Vienna, was finance minister of Austria in 1919 before he retired into academic life in Germany and the United States. David Mitrany came from beyond the borders of Hungary, born to a Jewish family in Bucharest. He moved as a young man across the continent first to England and then to the United States to reflect on the disintegration of the old European world from the successfully integrated New World.

From national to international integration

In successful attempts at national integration, as we have noted, formal changes in rules and structures had accompanied informal changes in markets, production, and communication: sometimes leading, sometimes lagging, but moving in the same direction. Some early optimistic supporters of postwar European integration, not only within Europe but also within the United States, saw a similar process then beginning on an international level, through which the creation of new political structures *and* the dynamics of trade and technical change would lead to a 'United States of Europe'.[18] As informal integration flowed on, across and beyond the boundaries of European nation-states, so new formal structures should and would be created to manage the new realities. Parallels between the prosperous and peaceful United States and the economically weak and conflict-ridden states of Western Europe were easy to make, particularly to Americans struck by the smallness of Western Europe and the apparent absurdity of the borders which divided it into national units, many scarcely viable.

Yet the nation-state *was* firmly established within the western half of Europe, as the primary focus of popular loyalty and decision-making authority. Paradoxically, the provision of Marshall aid, for all that it came with conditions requiring regional European cooperation far greater than any previously achieved, did much to reinforce the centrality of national authority for the citizens of each separate state, by providing the resources needed to extend social welfare and government intervention. Writing in 1957, Deutsch noted that 'most countries in the world today devote a larger part of their resources to their domestic economies, and a smaller part to their foreign trade, than they did half a century ago'; adding that 'the increase in the responsibilities of national government for such matters as social welfare and the regulation of economic life has greatly increased the importance of the nation in the lives of its members.'[19] Why then concern oneself, in the 1950s, with political integration above the level of the nation-state? There were two answers, both normative first and analytical second: the felt need to find ways of containing European rivalries without armed conflict, and the recognition that economic development increasingly required a framework of rules and regulations wider than those provided by individual European states.

Theories of political integration thus developed alongside political strategies of integration, feeding on one another as they grew. The closest symbiosis was between the 'neo-functionalist' school of Ernst Haas and his followers, and the promoters of European unification through the 'Community method'. The latter consisted of a Commission-led formulation of common policies, attracting the interests of economic and social elites from the national to the regional level, anticipating that successful identification and accumulation of common interests would 'spill over' into demands for further transfers of powers and into the progressive transfer of loyalties from national to regional-international institutions.[20] David Mitrany, writing during World War II about *A Working Peace System*, had looked to a diffusion of popular loyalties away from their concentration on the nation-state through the development of a network of functionally specific international institutions, rather than a transfer of those loyalties to a single new decision-making centre.[21] Karl Deutsch focused more on the interaction between social communication, central authority, and the development of political community both at the national and the international levels, attempting to measure the growth (or decay) of such socio-psychological communities, and to assess the factors which promoted their rise and fall.[22]

Common to all of these approaches was a concern for the relationship between the establishment of political structures and their legitimation through the development of a sense of shared interests and values, which Deutsch designated a political community. All assumed a close interaction between economic integration, creating new patterns of economic interest as well as of trade, the social communication which accompanied this – and which in part resulted from it – and the creation of new levels of political institutions. None was entirely clear as to which was the independent variable, which the dependent ones.

The central problem was the existence and underlying strength of the nation-state, with the anticipated and instinctive resistance of its leaders to the transfers of authority involved, and the strength of national loyalties which the experience of war had twice demonstrated. Mitrany did not satisfactorily answer the question of how national governments were to be persuaded to yield authority to international institutions, beyond preferring a less threatening multiplicity of functional rule-making organizations to the regional state which European federalists were proposing.[23] The neo-functionalists conceived of integration as a process which progressively eroded the authority of the nation-state, as 'political actors in several distinct settings are persuaded to shift their expectations and political activities to a new center'. They saw the process starting with such apparently unthreatening areas of policy as commercial relations and market regulation, and moving little by little, as loyalties transferred and demands for joint policy-making spilled over from one area to another, towards the most sensitive and symbolic areas of national sovereignty: foreign policy and defence.[24] But for this process to get under way, 'central institutions are required to represent the common interests which have brought the Member States together, and in order to accommodate such conflicts of interest as will inevitably arise.'[25] There is a degree of circularity here, in which the consent of national governments is required to establish institutions which will then operate, through the 'Community method' of Commission alliances with elite groups and organized interests, to undermine the authority of those same governments. De Gaulle as a political leader, and Stanley Hoffmann as an analyst, had little difficulty in exposing the weakness of the assumption that national governments would not resist the erosion of their sovereignty by technocratic elites, working to detach the loyalties of their citizens.[26]

It is easy to conclude, following Walker Connor's comment, that 'most of the theoretical writings on political integration have been characterized by an unwarranted degree of optimism' – about international integration as about national, assuming a unilinear process from non-integration to the creation of harmonious larger communities rather than the messy pulling and hauling of inter-group conflict over the location and control of the levers of authority.[27] Both Mitrany and Haas – and with Haas, many of the enthusiasts and idealists who staffed the European Commission in its early years – assumed that the careful pursuit of common interests would bring about an increasing harmony of perceived interests, rather than requiring more active management of divergent views.

Yet many of the concepts developed in the 1950s and early 1960s remain relevant and useful in attempting to understand the messy processes of regional integration within Western Europe. The link between social interaction, political decision-making and institution-building, and common identity or consciousness remains a central concern for theorists and for policy-makers.[28] Deutsch's distinction between 'amalgamation' and 'integration' draws attention to different degrees of centralization and decentralization in the creation of larger units of government, and of different degrees of compulsion and consent. Of these, the former is marked by strong central government, attempting if necessary to impose its authority on subordinate groups; the latter by limited transfers of power linked to the development of 'a sense of community and of institutions and practices strong enough and widespread enough to assure, for a "long" time, dependable expectations of "peaceful change" among its population.'[29] Looking at the Swiss and the American experiences, he noted the presence within the same unification movements of supporters of each of these two divergent goals. 'To encourage this profitable ambiguity, leaders of such movements have often used broader symbols such as "union", which would cover both possibilities and could be made to mean different things to different men.'[30]

'European union' has served as a rallying cry for supporters of political integration, and a symbolic threat to defenders of the nation-state. Never precisely defined, it allowed for supporters of a tightly institutionalized federal state and supporters of a loose confederation to come together in supporting intermediate objectives. But this convenient ambiguity has also made for much misunderstanding. In the first flush of revulsion against nationalism and nation-states after the war, committed 'Europeans' saw European union as *replacing* the failed nation-states out of which it would be built. After the recovery of national authority and prosperity, those who came from Western Europe's two most firmly established and centralized states, France and Britain, continued to see European union as the creation of a new European state, transferring sovereignty and identity *toute entière* from one level to another. Some, from the technocratic tradition of the French civil service, saw this transfer of authority as following the logic of industrial and technical change; others regarded it as necessary to counter the weight of the United States in an interdependent world. Many others, from within both France and Britain, saw such a development as an unacceptable threat to national sovereignty and identity.

Those who came from weaker or less firmly established states saw less of a structural contradiction between national and European levels of government, both because of their more conditional attachment to national sovereignty and because of the acceptance – in Germany, the Netherlands, and Italy – of the idea of government as the sharing of powers between different institutions, groups and levels of loyalty and authority. But in France and in Britain hopes and fears, ambitions and disappointments were easily exaggerated, because they were assessed in terms of a transition from the centralized nation-state to a powerful European state comparable to the transition from pre-industrial society to national government which both had witnessed in the nineteenth century. The ambiguity of the loosely defined objective of European union has made for similar misunderstandings in the United States, where assessments of progress towards European union tended to be placed within the context of the US's own mature national federation rather than of the diverse and multilingual confederation which – we will argue below – has been slowly emerging.

Economic integration, technical change

Systematic study of international economic integration is as novel as is comparable study of international political integration, and almost as intertwined with ideological assumptions and preferences. 'In the sense of *combining separate economies* into larger economic regions the word integration has a very short history ... No subject index of any book that I know on international economics prior to 1953 contains the entry "integration".'[31] Most economists regard

Jacob Viner's 1950 study of *The Customs Union Issue* as the first systematic treatment of the impact of such formal arrangements on the diversion and creation of flows of trade; though this in retrospect formed only one aspect of international economic integration, leaving out its financial, fiscal and distributional dimensions.[32] Theoretical concepts grew up alongside the development of the European Economic Community, with similar problems of circularity in generalizing from the particular and in the interaction and overlap between policy-makers and analysts. Most economists concerned with international integration in the 1960s and 1970s had played some part in the construction of Atlantic or West European institutions.[33]

The concept of a 'common market' was introduced to international economic law and to international economics by the Spaak Report in 1956 – a political exercise which necessarily skated over underlying differences about degrees of government intervention in the operation of markets and about the extent to which national economic policies were to be coordinated.[34] What lay beyond the clearing away of tariffs to establish a customs union was sketched out only loosely in the Treaty of Rome, in spite of the preamble's rhetorical commitment to 'concerted action in order to guarantee steady expansion, balanced trade and fair competition'. The theory of 'market integration' which has guided much debate in Britain and Germany is, Jacques Pelkmans has claimed, 'biassed against the mixed capitalist economy in its classical emphasis on *laisser faire* and its implicit belief in macro-economic stability'.[35] The United States model of an integrated economy has served, from the outset, as a point of reference for economic analysis of West European developments; but with much confusion and disagreement about the lessons to be drawn from the substantial size of the US federal budget, the interstate financial transfers which federal expenditure involves, or the importance (or unimportance) of the single currency and federal economic policies of the United States.

Above all, liberal macro-economics has found it difficult to estimate the dynamic effects of integration, as against the static benefits of removing barriers to trade: the inter-regional shifts in comparative advantage, the cumulative impact on the behaviour of firms, the creation and diversion of flows of investment. 'The whole issue of the so-called "dynamic" effects of integration is fraught with difficulty . . . economic analysis has not so far shown itself capable of throwing much light on it.'[36] European policy-makers have therefore been to a considerable extent 'flying blind' in economic integration, hitting areas of turbulence every time they grappled with issues on which underlying economic assumptions and ideological preferences diverged. Their difficulties have not, however, been peculiar to Europe: 'the lack of convergence in analytical views about how national economic policies influence each other is an impediment sufficiently severe to preclude ambitious efforts to coordinate economic policies' among the Group of 7, the OECD and – *a fortiori* – the IMF.[37]

The primarily static analyses of international trade theory and market integration can therefore provide little guidance in understanding the dynamics of European integration. We have to turn to political economists and students of technical change, noting with Joseph Schumpeter that 'it is not possible to explain *economic* change by previous *economic* conditions alone.'[38] The interaction of states and markets has been at the heart of political economy since the works of Smith, Hamilton, List and Marx. At the centre of the tension between the political and the economic order, Robert Heilbroner has argued, is a conflict between two logics of power. 'The logic of capital is essentially one of the expansion of value ... The logic of political power, by way of contrast, has always been concerned primarily with considerations of boundaries. It is the reach and limits of military and administrative power, not the possibilities of profit, that have guided the expansion of states.'[39] Markets constitute a powerful source of social and political change, and provoke similarly powerful reactions as societies and governments attempt to protect themselves against the impact of market forces: economic and political dynamics reacting with – and against – each other.[40]

The increasing pace of technological development has added a further dimension to the processes of economic integration. Schumpeter's vision of successive industrial revolutions 'each involving a unique combination of interdependent technical innovations closely related to accompanying managerial and organizational innovations and wider processes of institutional change' attracted little support in the long period of steady growth and apparently steady adaptation to new technology through the 1950s and 1960s.[41] Keynesian economics saw the growth of demand as a more fundamental factor, encouraging innovation which fed back into new patterns of demand without disrupting the underlying balance of the market. The 'widespread general neglect of the analysis of the technical change factor in macro-economics over the last decades', the underplaying of technological and managerial innovation as forces to which markets and governments find themselves compelled to adjust, may explain why conventional economics has so little to say about the dynamics of integration.[42]

The theoretical assumptions about economic integration which guided policy-makers through the early years of the European Economic Community were derived, as we have noted above, from established theories of international trade. Economists from outside the Anglo-Saxon tradition, particularly those in France and in Italy, held many reservations about the full applicability of theories of comparative advantage under open market conditions, and about the balance of advantage among different countries and regions which might emerge. But under conditions of sustained economic growth and rapidly rising international trade there was little incentive to question the principle of comparative advantage as such.

Experience since the early 1970s of recession, uneven development, structural adjustment, the growing importance of multinational companies in production and trade, the displacement of traditional trade patterns by foreign direct investment, the rise of Japan and other East Asian economies, have led some to conclude that 'today's world economy ... has outgrown the simple definition of free trade.'[43] As Patrick Minford has noted, a growing number of economists as well as policy-makers have concluded that 'the reigning paradigm' in international trade 'is embarrassingly at variance with the facts', leaving 'an extraordinary gap between international trade theory and international macroeconomics'.[44] Increasing evidence of imperfect competition, of oligopolistic markets, of the significance of intra-firm trade and of strategic partnerships between governments and companies in capturing new markets, has led to renewed attention being paid to the interaction between political intervention, company strategies, and market outcomes in the international economy.[45] The implications of this shift in perceptions for the pattern of European integration in the 1980s will be explored in the next chapter.

5

DIRECTION AND INDIRECTION: THE PROCESSES OF CHANGE

Optimism and pessimism have alternated in the debate over European integration. The first heady period of optimism of 1948–9, of rhetorical references to 'the United States of Europe', of the 'Congress of Europe' in the Hague and the formation of the Council of Europe, left behind it the European movement and the Strasbourg institutions. The second followed rapidly in 1951–2, with the successful launching for a smaller group of countries of the ECSC – to subside two years later with the collapse of the EDC proposals. The third, and so far most long-lived, followed the establishment of the EEC and Euratom. Sustained after the failure of the first enlargement negotiations by rapid progress in dismantling tariff barriers between the Six, and by the association of moves towards a common market with business confidence and strong economic growth, it collapsed into pessimism in the wake of the Luxembourg crisis and compromise of 1965–6.

The *relance* of the Hague summit of December 1969 was more soberly presented and received, leading to the successful accession of Britain, Denmark and Ireland, the launching of the first stage of the Werner Plan for Economic and Monetary Union by 1980, and the first hesitant developments of European Political Cooperation, before it ran into the sand in the transatlantic and international economic confusions of 1973–4.

Pessimism persisted from the mid-1970s until the mid-1980s; including – it should be remembered – the almost dismissive reception given on all sides to the ratification of the Single European Act, so much less of an institutional advance than its advocates had demanded and its opponents feared. Nor did the Commission's White Paper on 'Completing the Internal Market', a detailed programme couched in technical language, transform expectations when it was accepted by the Milan European Council in June 1985. The resurgence of optimism in 1987–8 was a change of mood – both inside and outside Western Europe – rather than a direct result of further formal initiatives: a recognition that integration *was* moving forward in several different dimensions in spite of the modesty of institutional innovation and the reservations of many member governments.

Looking back at the evolution of political, economic and social integration over the four decades since Winston Churchill declared the objective to 'build a kind of United States of Europe', in his speech to the University of Zurich in September 1946, it is possible to discern a more continuous process than that implied by these peaks and troughs of public expectations and political rhetoric. But that does not necessarily imply that the impetus has derived from the same mixture of forces throughout this period. The aim of this chapter is to explore the shifting dynamics which have pushed European integration forward, at a varying pace, up to the end of the 1980s. It stresses the importance of the American role in European development, first as sponsor, later as ambivalent senior partner. It notes the importance of formal institutions in shaping flows of interaction and habits of cooperation. It traces the increasing importance of informal flows, of economic and social trends, in transforming the shape of Western Europe during the difficult years of the 1970s. And it suggests that preoccupation with the challenges of technical change and of US and Japanese competition, as well as with the increasingly unsatisfactory nature of Europe's relations with America, have contributed significantly to the revival of initiatives for formal integration in the 1980s.

The shaping of the postwar structure
The political structure within which both the informal and the formal patterns of postwar West European integration developed was laid down by the region's dominant and defining power: the United States. The security provided by the Atlantic Alliance

69

stabilized Western Europe, and, extending its implicit protection over a fringe of neutrals, defined its boundaries. The Organization for European Economic Cooperation, in negotiation with its American sponsor and in parallel with the American-led GATT and IMF, set out the initial rules of economic interaction. The stability which set the context within which the Six could dare to move forward faster than their neighbours was the stability of the Atlantic framework. There can thus be no difficulty in discovering which came first within the postwar context, the informal flows or the formal rules. Postwar Western Europe grew up under America's leadership and America's protection, accepting American-sponsored rules of economic interaction and political cooperation.[1]

It was a measure of how deeply embedded the American-led structure of international economic cooperation later became that economic relations were seen, in the late 1950s and early 1960s, as matters for 'technical' – even 'technocratic' – negotiation and management, until de Gaulle reintroduced hard politics with his challenge to the role of the dollar within the Atlantic economic system. The functionalist distinction between the 'high' politics of defence and diplomacy and the 'low' politics of economic cooperation implied that economic competition and conflict were somehow less political and less sensitive than politico-military issues, in accordance with the liberal ideology of Anglo-Saxon economics. When in the late 1960s, and again in the late 1980s, American policymakers wished to remind European governments of the implicit postwar transatlantic bargain between military protection and economic cooperation, they found their European partners reluctant to accept that such a strategic trade-off had been made, let alone that it still obtained.[2]

The key institutional structures which shaped assumptions and encouraged and channelled informal flows across Western Europe in the first 15 years after World War II were *both* the Atlantic Alliance (and, from 1950 onwards, its integrated organization) and the OEEC. The two have to be seen together; the latter was an economic organization set up – like all economic institutions – for political reasons as much as economic, and supported implicitly by the extension of American military power. 'American leadership in the world political economy', after all, 'did not exist in isolation from NATO, and ... each was reinforced by the other.'[3]

The OEEC set the rules within which informal economic integration among West European countries could grow. Formally a European organization, with (at its foundation) 16 European member governments, it came into being in response to the Marshall Plan; the Act of Congress which authorized appropriations for the European Recovery Program included a rider that a permanent European organization should be established to guide Europe's path to recovery. At first American policy-makers hoped to persuade the countries of non-communist Europe to create their own federation, capable of sustained economic growth without long-term American assistance – and, many also hoped, without a long-term commitment of American troops. Rapidly recognizing that this could not win early acceptance, they next proposed a customs union: 'the formation of a single large market within which quantitative restrictions on the movement of goods, monetary barriers to the flow of payment and, eventually, all tariffs are permanently swept away' – as the head of the US Economic Cooperation Administration put it to the OEEC Ministerial Council in October 1949.[4]

If the British government, with the less vocal support of the Scandinavian and neutral countries, had not so vigorously resisted American pressures and preferences, a European economic space remarkably similar to that which has emerged in the 1980s would have become institutionalized 30 years earlier. With the British insisting on the priority of their American and global connections, the French turned to the problem of integrating a reviving Germany into a West European system which would not at the outset contain the United Kingdom as a counter-balance. Many of those who played a leading role in the construction of the Europe of the Six in the 1950s had devoted their energies in the immediate postwar years to the construction of a wider Western Europe, within this explicitly Atlantic framework: Spaak and Marjolin, in NATO and the OEEC respectively, and Monnet himself. Recognizing the extent to which their future prosperity and security depended upon a prosperous and stable West Germany; not taking for granted the temporary division of Germany or the preference which the Adenauer government then demonstrated for links with West Germany's Western neighbours; nor assuming with confidence that the postwar commitment to European defence which the American administration and Congress had made to meet the Soviet threat would necessarily be maintained for the foreseeable future – so French officials and politicians, with their colleagues from Belgium, Luxembourg and the Netherlands, grasped at the construction of more effective formal institutions, as a means of managing these intractable and overlapping problems.

There are alternative and competing versions of the development of the formal institutions of 'little' Western Europe from 1950 on. The more idealistic stress the importance of commitment and imagination from within the political elites of the six countries in creating and maintaining the impetus for supranational institutions, in spite of the resistance of the other member governments of the OEEC and the hesitations of many within the governments of the Six.[5] Those more persuaded of the underlying importance of patterns of power and influence look to the actions of successive American administrations, from Truman to Eisenhower and Kennedy, considering their consistent support for moves towards formal integration, and their repeated pressure on reluctant European national leaders to cooperate.[6]

Levels of economic and social interdependence were still relatively low, even though the dollar shortage had increased the importance of intra-European trade for each country's national recovery. Preoccupation with economic *recovery* to some extent obscured awareness of the demands and difficulties of technological change. All European economies after the war were uncompetitive with the American. But the aim of recovery was to modernize; and, until the late 1950s, faster rates of growth in Europe, the progressive adoption of methods of production developed in the United States between the wars, and continuing European advances in chemicals, engineering and aircraft manufacture suggested that a restoration of Western Europe's previous competitive position was attainable. American transfers of technology, most directly through the military offshore procurement programme, assisted in this hope. The British and the French built up comprehensive programmes of advanced research and development, both military and civil. They also developed successfully their own nuclear weapons, experimental nuclear power stations, jet aircraft and missiles; mostly a little behind the Americans but on occasion in parallel or even ahead.

The convergent influences that provided the impetus which carried formal European integration beyond the OEEC and the Council of Europe to the ECSC, and past the setback of the proposed European Defence Community (EDC) to Euratom and the EEC, thus came primarily from realist concern to create a more stable balance of power, and from idealist commitment to move away from national conflicts towards a more stable European order. There is of course no neat line to draw between one set of motivations and another. The containment of Germany within a tighter European framework was as much a political necessity as an ideal to many in the Netherlands, Belgium and France. The rhetoric served to persuade those involved that the enterprise was a noble one, not just an acceptance of the unavoidable.

Germany had been, since its unification in 1871, the natural hegemonic power in Europe, contained first by a patchwork of alliances and then by two destructive wars. The United States had been drawn into both wars, against its initial inclinations, to supply the countervailing forces needed; and found itself, after the second, the indisputable hegemon of Western Europe. But it had not been the intention of American policy-makers to remain heavily committed to the security of Europe for the indefinite future, to act as Europe's 'American Pacifier' – a substitute for constructing a self-sustaining European order.[7]

In the course of 1946–7 Washington recognized that the US commitment would have to be extended, until Western Europe had achieved the economic recovery which would enable it to sustain its own defence, and until the internal dynamics of the Soviet political system had mitigated its aggressive external stance. But that recovery could not be attained without rehabilitating the German economy, which in 1945–6 had been draining still further the scarce resources of its British and French occupiers. Nor could the burden of conventional defence, which continued to fall upon substantial numbers of American forces long after the initial hopes of rapid postwar demobilization had died, be shouldered by Western Europe without drawing upon its largest single contingent of manpower: the population of the Western zones of Germany. Hence the early postwar arguments among the three Western occupying powers about the treatment of the German economy; hence, above all, the intensity of American pressure for German rearmament when the outbreak of fighting in Korea appeared to confirm a direct Soviet military threat to Western Europe.

Germany's immediate Western neighbours would evidently have preferred a permanent American (and British) presence as their guarantee of security. But they had to take note of American intentions to limit the length and extent of their commitment, as of

American pressure to treat West Germany as a partner rather than an adversary; and they took increasing note of the potential instability of a divided Germany not closely linked to its Western neighbours, subject both to Soviet threats and to Soviet initiatives. Postwar German leaders for their part recognized the link between their recovery of autonomy and their acceptance of close formal links with their neighbours; the preamble of the 1949 'Basic Law' declares the *dual* resolve 'to preserve their national and political unity and to serve the peace of the world as an equal partner in a united Europe'.

If Britain had been willing to commit itself more fully to West European cooperation in 1949–50, the pattern of this cooperation in the 1950s and 1960s would have been substantially different. Britain could have provided the counterweight to a reviving Germany, in close partnership with France and the Benelux countries: the objective of the 1947 Dunkirk Treaty, echoing Anglo-French diplomacy of the 1930s and of the years before World War I. But Britain's economic and social links pulled it away from the European continent, whatever the political and strategic arguments for a reversal of roles. Only one-third of Britain's trade in 1950 was with the European continent, and the Scandinavian countries accounted for a substantial proportion of that; the sterling and dollar areas provided far more immediately attractive markets. Very few of the British population were yet familiar with the continent, beyond those who had experienced the fighting in 1944–5 and the subsequent occupation regime in Germany; wartime circumstances and the sterling area had oriented British trade and sentiment decisively away from Europe.

French politicians and officials, under pressure from their American sponsor, therefore turned from Britain to West Germany as the main focus for European partnership. Robert Schuman made the underlying purpose of the French government entirely clear in launching his 'Plan', in the atmosphere of high insecurity which followed the outbreak of the Korean war. 'La France ... a agi essentiellement pour la paix. Pour que la paix puisse vraiment courir sa chance, il faut d'abord qu'il y ait une Europe.'[8] If the United States could not be relied on to provide indefinite hegemonic leadership, if Britain would not commit itself and Germany was unacceptable as European hegemon, then the only alternative was a formal structure sufficiently tight to dispense with the need for a hegemon.

One should not, however, underestimate the importance of ideas, and idealism, in building the international coalitions and in creating the domestic support needed to carry the proposed transfer of authority to new institutions through governments and parliaments in six states. A revulsion against nationalism felt by many who had experienced defeat, occupation and imprisonment; appeals to common traditions of Christian democracy, of European socialism, of liberalism; the evocation of common 'European' themes of historical experience, culture and political ideas – all helped to supply symbolic justification for supporting the changes needed.[9] No matter that the intellectuals who promoted these European 'myths' presented a highly selective interpretation of European history, accenting the common threads and underplaying the conflicts and cruelties.[10] The intellectuals who had promoted the national myths which served to integrate nineteenth-century states had taken liberties at least as great with sordid reality. The legitimacy of European nation-states had been built out of the satisfaction of diverse interests, the effective performance of government and administration, and the cultivation of common symbols. The more limited legitimacy needed to support the authority of the new institutions proposed required in its turn its own set of myths and symbols, to justify the sacrifices of immediate interests which were essential for the system to operate.

The enthusiasm and optimism which marked the European movement in the postwar years, influencing journalistic comment and academic assessments and carrying over into popular perceptions both within Europe and within the United States, contained, however, a number of drawbacks. First, over-estimation of the popular strength of the intellectuals' 'European ideal', and under-estimation of the underlying solidity of the national framework of government, led some to pursue a strategy of amalgamation rather than of integration. The first draft of the Schuman Plan proposed to declare that 'L'Europe doit être organisée sur une base fédérale.' Watered down by more cautious advisers concerned to carry the proposals through a suspicious National Assembly, the published version still stated that 'cette proposition réalisera les premières assises concrètes d'une fédération européenne.'[11] American expectations and elite European hopes then attempted to commit West

European governments to a European Defence Community, together with the accompanying Political Community which was necessary to legitimize, control and finance it – a jump to strong central government well ahead of popular understanding or the development of a sense of shared political community.

The European Economic Community, picking up the drive to promote formal integration which had faltered with the French National Assembly's rejection of the EDC, was a more self-consciously limited proactive initiative. But the Commission in its early years included many who harboured the same hopes and objectives as in the early 1950s: many were, of course, the same people, a little older and wiser but with underlying predispositions unchanged. The struggle over competences which led up to the 'Luxembourg' crisis (and ensuing 'compromise') of 1965–6 was marked by attempts from the Commission to assert authority – and to accumulate the symbols of authority – well beyond what national electorates were yet likely to support, let alone against their own governments. The Commission was misled in its tactics by two other currents within this broad stream of enthusiasm and idealism: the optimistic assumption of underlying harmony of interests as integration proceeds, as against the sceptical acceptance that formal integration provides structures for containing conflict and bargaining over competing priorities; and the underestimation of the administrative strength and popular legitimacy of the reinvigorated national governments as against the claims of a new and supranational Commission.

A certain degree of overselling of the European idea and of the immediate objectives to be achieved was necessary to carry the proposals for positive new institutions past national parliaments and publics – as well as to motivate those who were working to promote them. The risk of overselling, however, is of subsequent disillusion when the product fails to perform to the specification promised. In some ways the promise of European integration was oversold even more in the USA than in Western Europe itself, to elites which too easily accepted the simile of a 'United States of Europe'. These elites understood only dimly the solidity of national governments who played an active role in the provision of services and welfare, and assumed too easily a natural harmony of West European interests under American leadership. The subsequent disillusion among American 'Europe-watchers' was all the higher, leading to a rapid decline of European studies in American universities and to a perception of Europe as having 'no trumps, no luck, no will' which lasted until the mid-1980s.[12]

It is difficult to assess how far the massive displacement of population which marked the war and its aftermath on the European continent provided an experience of social interaction which altered assumptions about shared interests and mental space. In the nature of the case, the many thousands of French and Dutch who did forced labour in wartime Germany, and the German and Italian prisoners who were posted to French farms until the farmers were demobilized, made their resentments more vocal than their other experiences and recollections. Collaboration, fraternization, had existed alongside resistance; and resistance had sometimes created its own *camaraderie* among those who had survived the camps and the clandestine routes across the occupied countries. Part of what bound the Six more closely together than their neighbours was the common experience of occupation, of the ebb and flow of refugees and of prisoners, of fighting men passing through their towns and villages. They experienced a common recognition (most vivid among the five countries which touched the Rhine and its tributaries) of the vulnerability of their boundaries, and shared the postwar predicament in which they found themselves.[13]

Economic recovery, institutional dynamics

There is a difficulty to be faced by any observer who tries to disentangle different influences over the evolution of both formal and informal integration in the period which followed the 'completion' of European recovery. It is that the institutional outcome – once again – was intended by many of the major players to be a different one, and that this time that different outcome was so nearly achieved. There was a relatively clear American strategy for adjusting the institutional patterns of European and Atlantic relations, set out most explicitly in President Kennedy's 'Interdependence Day' speech of 4 July 1962, but pursued by Washington from the late 1950s. There was a set of German priorities in security and economic issues, reflecting Federal Germany's restored status, revived economy, and rearmed forces. The British government was less certain, torn between its commitment to sovereignty and to the English-speaking world and its awareness of the implications for its long-term interests of institutional and economic changes within

Europe. British hesitancy, from the summer of 1962 on, allowed a French government which had learned to mistrust British approaches to European cooperation to assert *its* priorities without risking really severe condemnation from its partners.[14]

The American design, in keeping with the position of an enlightened hegemon, was for a two-pillar Atlantic Community, within which an institutionalized European Community would assume a greater share of the burdens and responsibilities which the USA had perforce carried until then. Pressure from within the West German government for greater influence and status in Western policy-making could thus be safely accommodated, contained within the dual structures of a united Europe and an Atlantic Community. In keeping with this design, considerable pressure was brought to bear on the British, under both the Eisenhower and the Kennedy administrations, to apply to join the European Community, to bring together all America's major European partners within a single formally integrated structure.[15] Both Dutch and West German support for British entry reflected the concern of these countries to maintain the closest possible US commitment to Western Europe, with British entry seen as likely to reinforce that two-way commitment.[16] The French government, together with a minority of German Christian democrats, was alone in questioning the optimistic assumption that the interests of a more tightly-integrated Western Europe and of its Atlantic patron would prove harmonious, rather than divergent.

Thus far a justification could be made for an explanation of institutional development in terms of hegemonic leadership – except that the French government successfully defied the hegemonic leader and its major partners, and went on to challenge the claimed authority of the European Community as such. Idealists saw the Luxembourg crisis as a major defeat for the Commission, and therefore for European integration as such. The Commission itself defiantly maintained its commitment to build 'the European Federation', calling on 'the European people as a whole' and 'the major social groups within the Community' to move with it ahead of their national governments.[17] Those academics and enthusiasts who had identified the strengthening of the authority of the Commission as against national governments with the advance of European integration took its cries of pain to be evidence of real disintegration, and concluded that the formal integration of Europe was now to be a matter of stumbling steps rather than of confident strides.

With hindsight, a closer look at political and economic trends suggests a more complex pattern of developments. Institutional patterns *had* helped to shape attitudes and outcomes. The establishment of the European Communities as a focus for authoritative and effective decision-making over a limited range of policy areas brought together an increasing number of national ministers, officials and interest-group representatives. Once assembled, these people exchanged information and opinions on subjects beyond their immediate agenda, and acquired habits of constructive bargaining as they were socialized into continuing groups. The linking together within a formal framework of rules and rule-making of the geographically and economically central countries of Western Europe, in the pursuit of a range of economic and political objectives, changed the context within which their neighbours approached international cooperation. Early success in sustaining high rates of growth and rapid increases in intra-Community trade augmented the Community's attraction for other European OECD members. The British government rapidly found that the loose structures of the European Free Trade Area, set up under British leadership in response to the establishment of the EEC in 1957–8, were of only marginal utility; partly because the other members were of only secondary importance to Britain in economic and political terms, once the economies of West Germany, France and the Low Countries had been rebuilt. But a working political and economic entity which brought together Britain's largest European neighbours and trading partners, with apparent benefits distributed among its members, posed a challenge to British foreign policy as such – as it did to other West European countries outside the original Six.

Economic and technical change was also beginning to push West European countries together: reluctantly and experimentally in the early 1960s, but indicating the likely direction of change. Britain and France had experienced greater and greater difficulties in financing their full military and civil research programmes in the late 1950s, and even more problems in competing with larger US expenditures. In the course of the 1960s, as observed in Chapter 4, they looked first to each other, then to Germany, as a bilateral partner. This was the pursuit of collaboration, not of integration. Industrial concentration in Britain and France in the 1960s was a matter of merging separate companies into state-supported 'national champions', in limited cooperation with other national champions. Transnational production, let alone the creation of transnational consortia, was still beyond the bounds of political acceptability or perceived economic necessity.

In other industrial sectors trade was increasing rapidly, but production remained largely national. Most of the multinational companies which operated in Europe in the 1960s allowed their national subsidiaries to have considerable autonomy, recognizing the particular national environments within which they operated. Ford of Britain became a fully owned subsidiary in 1961, buying out its minority local shareholders; but it continued to build a very different range of cars from Ford of Germany for a decade more. Philips was expanding, and buying its way into other national markets; but the degree of central control and of centrally coordinated production remained limited. Unilever adapted its production, products and marketing to the idiosyncratic habits and demands of each set of national consumers.

Social integration also remained firmly linked to each national setting, despite all the efforts of town-twinning schemes and the hopes of functional theorists. Mass tourism was only just beginning to cross national frontiers; the motorways and airports which were to carry the flow were under construction, or were still being planned. Those national officials who travelled between their capitals and Brussels in increasing numbers as the 1960s progressed did so by train or (most often) by propeller-driven plane, their journeys retaining much of the excitement – and the frustrations – of foreign travel. Frontier checks remained in force, frontier posts the occasion for queues and official inspections. The removal of tariff barriers preceded the dismantling of many other barriers, both formal and informal; the construction of formal institutions moved well ahead of the popular integration which idealists had hoped would accompany it.

Institutional lourdeur, informal integration
Formal integration moved forward, with only brief halts and setbacks, after the Luxembourg crisis. Between 1969 and 1979 the European Community admitted three new members and opened negotiations with three more; initiated a three-stage plan for

economic and monetary union, and recovered from the collapse of that plan to launch a more modest European monetary system; developed a framework for 'European Political Cooperation' along-side the Community; and established a Regional Development Fund to alleviate some of the greater inequalities in an enlarged Community.

Yet the overall impression, inside as well as outside the European Community, was of institutional ineffectiveness and *lourdeur*.[18] Increasingly, the major European governments dealt with each other and with the United States through channels outside the formal structures of the European Community. The most significant of these, from 1974, were the annual Western Economic Summits, attended by four of the Community's heads of government and – after some hard lobbying by the smaller member states – by the President of the European Commission. Ideas inhibited adjustment in Community priorities and policy, as the enthusiasts of the Commission and the veterans of Community building defended the *acquis communautaire*, and the integration theology, of the 1960s against the changing circumstances of the 1970s. Institutions appeared less effective, as the first generation of committed Commission officials began to tire and retire, and the skills of the Commission in producing workable proposals which could command the assent of *nine* member governments appeared limited.[19]

Many of the uncertainties of West European policy-making during the 1970s stemmed from the increasing ambiguity of the assumed relationship between West European and Atlantic cooperation. The failure of the American 'Grand Design' of 1961–3, seeking to create an Atlantic Community within which an integrated Western Europe would develop a balanced partnership with the United States, had left disappointed expectations, and resentments, on both sides of the Atlantic. Divergence of views between the French government and its European partners over how best to handle transatlantic relations undermined European cooperation on issue after issue. American impatience with European unwillingness either to shoulder a greater share of the global security burden, or to follow Washington's leadership, or to adjust in the USA's favour the rules of an international economy which the French government still believed to be structurally biased in that direction, encouraged a degree of unilateralism: an insistence that the Europeans accept the American definition of their shared interests.

So the American suspension of dollar convertibility in August 1971 was justified by the refusal of the European allies – and Japan – to accept alternative ways of relieving the strains on the US economy. The failure to agree on a multilateral adjustment of exchange rates, and the consequent shift to a floating rate regime, derailed the Werner Plan for Economic and Monetary Union before it had reached the end of its first stage. The 1973–4 'Year of Europe' represented another American-led attempt to redefine the understood conditions of the Atlantic bargain, with Henry Kissinger explicitly stressing the distinction between US 'global' responsibilities and the Europeans' 'regional' role.[20] The emerging (and still largely ineffective) structure of European Political Cooperation was a particular source of concern in Washington, with the administration requesting that its officials should be allowed to sit in on its discussions in order to ensure that European and American views coincided. The growing self-confidence of successive German governments was a further preoccupation. Germany's role as a loyal junior partner in the 1960s, but an increasingly independent actor as the 1970s progressed, was demonstrated first in the pursuit of *Ostpolitik* and later in the disputes over the proposed deployment of enhanced-radiation weapons and over the modernization of intermediate-range nuclear weapons.

But alongside increasing concern about institutional 'blockage' and the shift of attention by the major European governments away from the institutions of Brussels and towards Atlantic, European and bilateral summit meetings, the flow of informal integration was gradually changing the context within which European governments operated. Across continuing barriers to investment, European companies and retail chains were beginning to emerge. General Motors and Ford progressively integrated their European production and marketing in the course of the 1970s, with components produced or procured across the continent. The proportion of GNP accounted for by trade was rising in all West European countries; and so was the proportion of trade accounted for by intra-European trade. With the gradual adjustment of the British economy to Community membership, and the increasing preponderance of the West German economy within the region, patterns of European trade were converging around a single core. The D-mark was becoming established within a world of floating exchange rates as the key European currency. *Modell Deutschland* now provided the most important impetus to European economic development.

The passage of people back and forth across West European borders was increasing year by year. Tourist flows within Europe rose from 40 million cross-frontier arrivals in 1960 to over 80 million in 1970, and to 160 million in 1980.[21] Business travel and political and official consultations were rising in parallel.[22] The spread of direct telephone dialling across Western Europe and the proliferation of television channels overlapping national frontiers helped to pull the region further together; by 1980 the cable networks in Belgium and the Netherlands were providing over a dozen channels in four languages. With the rise of cross-border interaction of all kinds, from intermarriage to second-home ownership to aircraft movement to crime, national governments found themselves forced to adjust legal and administrative arrangements. The establishment of the Pompidou Group in 1971 within the framework of the Council of Europe to combat the drugs trade, and of the Trevi Group in 1976 within the framework of European Political Cooperation to coordinate national efforts in combating terrorism, provide classic examples of responsive formal integration, bringing interior ministries and intelligence agencies into the network of West European coordination for the first time. The strike of lorry-drivers on the frontiers of France and Italy in February-March 1984, in protest at the delays caused by customs checks and national documentation, provides an equally classic example of the evolution of informal trends building up pressure on national governments to change formal rules.[23]

Technical change and institutional adaptation

Formal structures and boundaries, once set up, allow and encourage the strengthening of informal interactions along the channels created – or across the space thus cleared and enclosed. The external crises and disturbances which buffeted Western Europe throughout the 1970s made for a general defensiveness of response, both institutionally and politically. Those who had built the structures of formal West European integration in the 1950s and 1960s, under conditions of sustained economic growth, American benevolence, and ample supplies of raw materials and energy, concentrated on maintaining what they had established as best they could in far more adverse circumstances.

But, alongside the debilitating arguments about agricultural policy and the Community budget, officials and ministers found themselves using the channels of communication and negotiation provided by the formal structures of European cooperation to handle new issues as they arose. These ranged from environmental pollution to technological collaboration, from the management of political and economic crises in Eastern Europe to the military and technological challenges posed by the Reagan administration's SDI initiative. Rising generations which knew World War II only as history flowed along Europe's motorways and through its airports, grumbling about the inconveniences imposed by national air control systems and passport controls. The strains of industrial adjustment and economic recession pushed member governments into joint programmes of restructuring, and into hard negotiations in defence of European interests and markets with the US administration and within the multilateral frameworks of OECD and GATT.[24] Beneath the atmosphere of gloom at the failure to achieve any of the major steps forward proposed during the 1970s, or to manage the processes of economic adjustment as successfully as the USA or Japan, the 'Europe des petits pas' continued to shuffle forward, through the incremental accumulation of private actions and governmental reactions.

With the benefit of hindsight it is possible to trace the recovery of momentum in formal integration which became evident in the late 1980s, and to find its origins at the beginning of the decade. Many of the early moves were far more responsive than proactive. Renewed efforts to strengthen European Political Cooperation began with the embarrassing failure to coordinate European responses to the Soviet invasion of Afghanistan, in December 1979, or to American demands to support their reaction. Crises in Poland and Iran increased the urgency of West European coordination and the awareness of divergent perspectives across the Atlantic; the arrival of the Reagan administration, the fourth change in the US Presidency in nine years, and the added complications of the Lebanon, raised consciousness further. The revival of the Franco-German defence dialogue in 1982, the London and Genscher-Colombo Reports on reinforcing EPC, the shift towards WEU by the larger members, were the result of preoccupied policy-makers using the institutional mechanisms available to handle urgent and difficult issues – not of any long-term strategy or premeditated plan.[25] Gradual rises in activity within the Trevi and Pompidou groups, and increasing cross-border cooperation among European police forces, were similarly responsive measures. In 1987 the pressure of regional information exchange within Interpol led to the establishment of a separate European office to handle the flow.[26]

Recognition of the extent to which West European interests now diverged from those of the United States, and of the necessity to manage relations with a transatlantic ally no longer certain of its hegemonic position or of the identity of its global and national interests, contributed to the pressures which pushed West European governments together – on the whole reluctantly, with many hesitations and mixed motivations. German and British political leaders saw the revival of WEU as a means of increasing West European influence within an integrated alliance; the Spanish government saw WEU entry as a means of persuading its electorate to accept membership within the alliance, by giving it a stronger European – as opposed to Atlantic – image. French governments were as anxious about a weakening of the American commitment of conventional forces to Europe as they were about the technological challenge posed by SDI and the financial dislocations threatened by the rising US trade deficit. Other areas of disagreement between Europe and the US included disputes over trade and trade policy, differences over global economic management, European concern at the shifts in American policies on nuclear weapons, East-West relations, the Middle East, and all the shock of the Reykjavik superpower summit of October 1986. A widening agenda thus brought European ministers and officials together to discover that their common interests were closer than those which they shared with the USA.

The European Community itself emerged from a tangled set of negotiations on enlargement, containment of the CAP, and budgetary costs and benefits, in 1983–4. Immensely costly in time and ministerial attention, and often bitter, the arguments over the linked issues of the CAP and the budget nevertheless moved the Community away from the old orthodoxies – and helped to persuade member governments that the Community's unwieldy decision-making arrangements must be adapted. The prospect of the accession, in January 1986, of a further two states was conclusive. The negotiations which led to the Single European Act were completed in time for the Luxembourg European Council of December 1985: its acceptance of extended majority voting and strengthened powers of initiative for the Commission reflecting rather less the enthusiastic pressures for European union from within the European parliament than acceptance of the necessity of more efficient procedures for the pursuit of shared interests through common decision in a Community of Twelve.[27]

Unease about the slowness of European adjustment to the succession of economic shocks of the 1970s sparked off a range of private and public responses. Arguments that the economies of West European countries were over-regulated and over-taxed, and thus unable to respond rapidly to changes in the economic environment, were at first resisted by many continental governments. The failure of the French socialist government's attempted dash for national economic recovery, in 1982–3, as well as growing acceptance of the evidence of 'Eurosclerosis', made for a convergence of perspectives on economic management, pointing towards deregulation and away from active governmental direction of national economies. The approach adopted by the British government from 1979–80 on was echoed by the French right, at first in opposition and then, from March 1986, in government. The approach was also echoed, more remarkably, by the socialist government of Spain, while fainter echoes could be heard in policies in the Netherlands, Germany and Italy. This general shift from intervention and corporate sponsorship towards deregulation and adjustment to changes in the international market provided the intellectual (or ideological) and political support for the Commission's programme, launched in June 1985, for the 'completion' of the internal market by 1992.

Alongside this, however, can be traced another response, much more in the interventionist and corporatist tradition of European economic management. Concern over the capability of European industry to compete with American multinational companies, supported by their government in the penetration of international markets and (above all through defence procurement) in technological research and development, had marked French attitudes to European integration from the 1960s on. The general failure of the national champion strategy which all major European governments had adopted in technologically advanced industries was becoming evident by the late 1970s. The rise of Japan, and the potentially revolutionary impact of electronics and of information technology on patterns of international trade and competition, impressed themselves progressively on Europe's leading companies and on many within the Commission and within member governments.

Here again one can cite no single motivating force, no heroic leader or critical turning-point. It has been the convergence of private and public interests, of national strategies and Commission ambitions, combined with a changing intellectual climate and, above all, the evident impact of technical change itself, which has made for the accumulation of initiatives and innovations in policy. The Danish Prime Minister's declaration, in September 1988, that 'the evolution of Europe in the next decades' would be shaped by 'the phasing in of the information society to replace the industrial culture and industrial technology which have served us so well for almost two hundred years' – that Europe was facing a technological divide which its American and Japanese competitors were better prepared to cross – had been far from the conventional wisdom of most national political systems within Europe at the beginning of the decade.[28] 'There appears', as Michael Blumenthal has observed, 'to be a fundamental lag between the current rate of technological change and the rate of adjustment to these changes among decision-makers ... The problem is further complicated because the private sector accepts technological change more rapidly than the governments.'[29]

An alliance between M. Davignon, appointed Commissioner for Industry, and the leaders of several of Western Europe's largest industrial and technological companies, led in 1979 to the creation of the European Round Table.[30] This coalition of private and public interests, the former lobbying national governments to support the programmes the latter proposed to them, led to the launching of the ESPRIT programme for European cooperation in information technology in 1982; and, less directly, to the proliferation of Community-sponsored collaborative programmes in the years which followed – FAST, BRITE, STAR, RACE, JESSI. The model for these initiatives was more that of the government-industry partnerships orchestrated by MITI than of the technocratic planning on the French model which had inspired the Community in the 1960s; though it might also be argued that these programmes represented an adaptation of the characteristically French approach to the Japanese challenge.[31]

The French government was one of the first to press for a concerted Community response to 'the electronic revolution', calling in a memorandum which it circulated to other Community members in September 1983 for 'un espace industriel européen' to reverse the increasing 'technological dependence' of European firms on American and Japanese firms in high technology.[32] The French response to SDI was to propose an alternative European programme to promote collaboration in related technologies: EUREKA, ostensibly civilian in its orientation, but bringing together the major European defence procurement companies, in private joint ventures which attracted public support. The German government was open to such proposals, with the *Land* governments of Bavaria and Baden-Württemberg – in particular – pursuing strategies of public-private partnerships in high technology in sectors which appeared to require a more defined European dimension.

Part of the learning curve which pushed these governments together was their common commitment to Airbus Industrie, mounting an increasingly successful challenge to American domination of the civil aircraft market in the early 1980s, with government subsidy and support; and to the European space programme, which after many years of disappointments began in the 1980s to challenge the USA in the commercial launching of satellites.[33] After the agonizing transatlantic disputes over the management of industrial surplus capacity, in steel and in chemicals, this demonstration of the ability to compete in some advancing sectors was welcome: for a mixture of motives, from pride in technical advance to improvement in trade balance to awareness of the links between technological capabilities and future military capacity. There was also the experience of American attempts to tighten controls over the transfer of technology to hostile powers, by intervening extraterritorially to prevent European licence-holders from supplying equipment for the Soviet-West European gas pipeline, and by blocking a number of other civil contracts with the USSR and Eastern Europe. These only strengthened the resolve of those in European companies, in the Commission, and in national governments who were setting out to build a European network in high technology less dependent on cooperation with the USA and Japan.

Behind these successive initiatives lay a shift in the intellectual climate, resisted by many of those who were most vigorously promoting strategies of deregulation and reduced government intervention, welcomed not only by the traditional supporters of industrial interventionism but also by many in private industry who were struggling to compete with the USA and Japan. The argument that 'interstate competition' was shifting 'from competition in land to competition for technology' had a powerful appeal to those who saw American use of strategic export controls and Japanese partnership between government and business as strategies aimed at creating comparative advantage in rapidly-changing and oligopolistic global markets.[34] While disillusionment with Keynesian approaches to economic management, in the wake of the inflation and instability of the 1970s, had led to a return to classical and monetarist approaches to policy, this analysis pointed to a structural approach, which argued that 'certain types of technical change ... have such widespread consequences for all sectors of the economy that their diffusion is accompanied by a major structural crisis of adjustment, in which social and institutional changes are necessary to bring about a better "match" between the new technology and the system of social management of the economy.'[35]

The 'growing gap between the reality of economic integration and the conceptual and political framework in which we are used to think about it' has been noted in the previous chapter.[36] In their public declarations Europe's political leaders found themselves more comfortable with the deregulatory response than with the strategic trade response; though in their acceptance of successive collaborative programmes, as well as in many of their policies at national and regional levels, they demonstrated their sympathy for the strategic approach. The Commission itself was not entirely coherent in its approach, with those responsible for competition policy, external relations, and industrial policy, research and technology on occasion pulling in different directions. But the stress on improving Europe's competitiveness in global markets which pervaded all Commission documents in the late 1980s went well beyond the clearing away of remaining obstacles to a full internal market. 'The invisible hand', as M. Delors put it, 'is itself in need of guidance.' American analyses of trade policy as a strategic game were well understood in Brussels; Paul Krugman, one of its leading exponents, contributed a conceptual chapter on economic integration to the 1987 Padoa-Schioppa Report.[37]

Advisers and actors had differing strategies, emphasizing approaches that were monetarist or structuralist, deregulatory or collaborative, according to their particular predispositions. Governments more often responded to uncertain developments in the light of conflicting advice and evidence. Arguments between Community member governments over financial deregulation and monetary coordination – and plans for monetary union – continued while electronic innovation integrated global financial markets, and imbalances between the USA and Japan transformed the context for policy: theories and regulations jeopardized by shifting capabilities and practices in the markets, within Western Europe as well as outside. Uncertainty over developments in the global economy, over trends towards a concentration of economic power in three regions or towards a dispersion of competition in the direction of newly industrializing states, made for hesitant advances in policy. The unavoidable overlap between security and economic considerations made for even greater hesitancy, in a period when so many aspects of both were changing rapidly.

The resurgence of the late 1980s should not therefore be seen as the simple outcome of any far-sighted Commission strategy – however far-sighted and strategic some within the Commission (and some national governments) attempted to be. Nor should it be seen as the consequence of the ratification of the Single European Act – a useful but modest revision of the Treaty of Rome – or of the adoption of the Commission's 1992 programme. The 'sorcerer's apprentice' development of the 1992 programme, with most governments surprised by the gathering impetus of the process they had themselves set in motion, suggests that many other impulses gave it additional momentum. The importance of developments in West European foreign policy cooperation, security consultation, and military procurement – often neglected by those who focus on integration as an economic and market phenomenon – has been indicated above. So has the significance of external political, security, economic and technological challenges, to which so many of these innovations in formal integration responded. Informal integration within the 'West European space' had created new demands for the adjustment of rules and the management of policy, moving ahead of these formal processes for the first time since the postwar initiation of European integration.

American and Japanese observers, overcoming their earlier scepticism about the policy-making capacities of West European institutions, were persuaded at the end of the 1980s that they were watching the construction of a stronger Europe. Optimism had returned to the debate within the Community, while its European neighbours were being drawn towards the Community and were reconsidering their relations with it. Despite successive declarations on European identity and European union, however, the shape and extent of that 'Europe' and the sense of community and shared values which should give it legitimacy has remained unclear – has, indeed, been becoming increasingly unclear as the relationship between the EC and EFTA has grown closer, and as the politics and economic orientation of the Community's eastern neighbours have begun to shift.

6

FORTY YEARS ON

Writing about the 'enduring balance' between the two alliance systems in Europe in the 1970s, when both the East-West and the West-West relationships were 'in as exemplary a state of stability as anything can be in a revolutionary world', Anton De Porte warned that stability is only 'a special case of change, not the natural order of things'.[1] Looking back from the perspective of 1990, it is possible to trace more clearly the impact of the cumulative changes – political, economic and social – that have developed within the stable institutional and security frameworks which the postwar order provided. As the dividing lines imposed by this order weaken, many old familiar images are re-emerging. But they re-emerge within the context of a continent transformed by economic and social integration, and reshaped by the construction of formal institutions.

It is an open question how far the continent has also been transformed through political integration – through the development of a sense of shared community wider than the nation-state, sufficient to support the burden of economic redistribution and common rule-making which the political agenda of the 1990s may demand. A diffuse sense of European identity has emerged throughout Western Europe; but the geographical extent of that shared community remains loosely defined, and the obligations and commitments to which such a sense of community might lead have not been tested. It is here that the role of politics is central. Ideas, images, mental maps are shaped and reshaped by the rhetoric of political leadership as well as by the pressure of external events and the flow of communication and social interaction. The romantics and intellectuals who defined (and embellished) national histories and communities in the course of the nineteenth century marked out the lines on which Europe was reshaped, and provided the rationale for the sovereign authority their rulers – or would-be rulers – claimed. There are, as I have argued in Chapter 2, a great many definitions of 'Europe' available for intellectuals and politicians (in power and out of power) to call on as rationales for their preferred strategies. We may anticipate that some of the central political conflicts of the 1990s within Europe will revolve around these competing definitions and the implications which follow from accepting them.

Political leadership and political ideas, interacting with socio-cultural identities and communities, represent a field where prediction is impossible and anticipation difficult. But politicians, and the publics to which they appeal, operate within the constraints imposed by external commitments and pressures, economic developments, and social trends. The strategic stability provided by the structure of the two competing alliances and the institutionalization of American leadership of 'the West' have set the context within which European politics, institutions, and economic and social interdependence have developed over the past 40 years. The loosening of that strategic security framework in the course of the 1970s and 1980s, as West European priorities and attitudes diverged from American ones, made for greater autonomy of developments in both informal and formal West European integration. Its further loosening in the 1990s will give more play to the economic and social trends which are pushing the countries of Europe together – unless the re-emergence of local conflicts from under the blanket of superpower alliance leadership begins to tear some of them apart. It will also leave the formal institutions of Western Europe, which grew up within the shadow of American political and economic hegemony, to play an increasingly autonomous role – quite possibly the determining role – in the future political development of Europe as a whole.

Western Europe, core Europe
The transformation of Western Europe and the transformation of

wider Europe are inextricably linked. The evident prosperity and technical advance of Western Europe have pulled the countries of Eastern Europe westwards. The combination of political stability, limited government, social partnership and economic success has provided a West European model to which intellectuals and dissidents in Eastern Europe have referred, in evident contrast to the failures of the East European order. Western Europe had spilled over into Eastern Europe increasingly as the 1970s moved into the 1980s, with television broadcasts following radio, with West European tourists and businessmen accentuating the contrast between success and failure.

The imbalance between Western and Eastern Europe is fundamental to Europe's future development. Western Europe represents an organized economic space, with politically coherent structures to manage it; Eastern Europe a collection of poorly integrated economies, politically disunited. The core of Europe is indisputably within Western Europe. The reopening of the old links between 'West Central' and 'East Central' Europe will serve to confirm this rather than making for any major shift in the balance. In retrospect the cutting off of Eastern Europe can be seen not as having damaged the West German and West European economies, but as having diverted their thrust west and south (as the sixteenth-century advance of the Turks similarly redirected European economic links), to the benefit of the Atlantic regions, and of Spain and Portugal. The new governments of Eastern Europe are asserting their determination to 'rejoin the West' more than to design some new pan-European order. We face, as Pierre Hassner has remarked, 'not the Finlandization of Western Europe which Americans feared, but the Brusselization of Eastern Europe'.[2]

West Germany on its own had re-emerged as the central pivot of the European economy, of European politics, even to some extent of European social interchange (as noted in Chapter 2), well before the issue of reintegration with the GDR had moved from the sphere of political rhetoric to that of realistic possibility. The strategic centrality of Germany to Europe had been evident, after all, since 1870; the rationale for the Franco-British *Entente* of 1907, as much as for the attempted Franco-British coalitions of 1947–9 and 1970–73, was to provide – under different political circumstances – an effective counterbalance to an otherwise predominant Germany.[3] Repeated American pressure on Britain to accept a more active role in an institutionalized political Western Europe stemmed from the same perception: that Germany was the key to Europe, and that the full engagement of France and Britain was needed to lock a divided Germany into the West and to guard against the potentially disruptive impact of a future reintegration with its Eastern zone.

Successive British governments argued in return that the Atlantic security framework, institutionalized in NATO, was the key to the containment both of the Soviet threat and of the German problem, and that the French pursuit of West Germany was an attempt to undermine the Atlantic Community. The Franco-German relationship as de Gaulle envisaged it *did* threaten the Atlantic security framework, leaving his German *interlocuteurs* to balance uneasily between Atlantic and European alternatives. But as French *intransigeance* has moderated and the balance of governmental interaction has shifted across the whole range of policy towards a West European framework within a broader and looser Western grouping, so British reluctance has left the Franco-German relationship to become the political core of Europe, with the Benelux countries and the Italians adding their weight to the balance. The relative decline of the British economy over the past 30 years has also contributed to the re-establishment of German centrality – the two counterpoles of European economic interdependence in the late 1950s giving way to an integrated European economy with a single core. Western acceptance of the centrality of Germany within the European polity and economy has been reflected in the gradual shift in assumptions in West European capitals about the linked questions of German reintegration and European reintegration over the past two decades. A widely held belief that German unification was incompatible with *West* European integration, posing *Ostpolitik* and *Westpolitik* as alternatives, has become a recognition that the integration of East Central Europe into the West European core is the necessary and long-term process which brings the different parts of Germany safely back together.

The Community system, the institutional core
The six-country European Economic Community was not from its formation the central institutional focus for intergovernmental bargaining and rule-making in Western Europe. The failure of the EDC proposals had made its negotiators more cautious; economic

integration was thus to be pursued without direct or explicit linkage to political and security considerations. The competing grand designs of de Gaulle and the Kennedy administration in 1961–3 both envisaged that it should develop into such a focus; but the failure of these incompatible designs left an Economic Community coordinating only part of Western Europe's economy. The growth of the Franco-German relationship, the progressive enlargement of the EC, the successive addition of new issues to the Community agenda and the development of associated structures to grapple with such most sensitive issues as foreign policy, security, and threats to domestic order, have built up a multilateral framework within which the governments of Western Europe now make much of the policy which was formulated by separate national governments, under American leadership, two generations ago. Much of this development, as we have seen, has been responsive rather than proactive, following the impetus of informal trends rather than the rhetoric of repeated commitments to pursue European union. But rhetoric and responses have interacted, in justifying successive packages of rules and in shaping the institutions through which they are implemented.

Forty years after the Schuman Plan, those who pushed ahead with a more tightly integrated political and economic community in the hope that they would draw their more reluctant neighbours behind them have thus had that hope amply fulfilled. In 1958 the member states of the EEC accounted for some 54% of European OEEC production. In 1988 the enlarged EC accounted for over 80%, and was in active negotiation with the EFTA governments, which accounted for almost all the remainder, about the rules which should govern their access to Community markets and the constitution of their shared European economic space. The countries of southern and eastern Europe have been drawn in their turn towards this expanding integrated economy; with a hierarchy of association agreements linking the states of the EC's Mediterranean periphery, and with the EC's eastern neighbours jostling for priority in the queue for financial and technical assistance and market access. The Community's response necessarily involves its major governments taking into account their political and security concerns as well as their economic interests. As a vehicle for collective action, the Community has thus been transformed from an instrument of Franco-German reconciliation into the key power structure in Europe: a structure of collective leadership, to replace the unacceptable single hegemon which a revived Germany would otherwise have threatened to become.

In the Atlantic system within which Western Europe grew together, the United States as the predominant power set the rules and provided a disproportionate share of the public goods of money and credit, economic assistance, political and military security. In the European system which has been emerging into autonomy, the rules are set by multilateral bargaining among the major players within the context of established formal institutions. Economic redistribution, through the Community budget and its regional and agricultural policies, has been a focus of hard multilateral bargaining throughout the 1980s, which will become all the more intense in the 1990s as the claimants of economic assistance from eastern and southern Europe press their case and as the prosperous EFTA countries are drawn more directly into the process of redistribution. Monetary policies are at present the focus of intensive negotiation, in the wake of the Delors Report on Economic and Monetary Union and the preparations for the intergovernmental conference proposed for 1990–91. Only the provision of security has remained an area in which West European countries depend substantially on America's contribution to collective goods, with the formal institutions of West European security cooperation still subordinated to the Atlantic Alliance as part of the bargain which has maintained the US military commitment to Europe. Here too, however, there has been a gradual shift of emphasis, with European Political Cooperation and Western European Union becoming fora for autonomous coordination of European policies.

After the pessimistic appraisals of five to ten years ago, what is striking about the formal institutions of West European integration at the beginning of the 1990s is their strength and solidity. Rules are laid down across an expanding agenda, in many areas by majority vote; levels of compliance within the member states compare with those observable within the different states of the USA a few decades ago. Community rules, indeed, now carry well beyond the Community's boundaries. They are adopted as a necessary counterpart to market access by the EFTA associates of the European economic space, in a pattern which is likely to spread further across eastern and southern Europe as those regions draw closer to Europe's prosperous and powerful core.

Many of the features of the European Community of 1990 would immediately be recognizable to the proponents of European union of 40 years ago: central institutions with broad competences and policy-making powers, an extending framework of European law, intense interaction among national governments through these institutions, a European parliament now directly elected, and a progressive expansion of membership to bring most of Western Europe within this framework of institutional rules. But many of the other features which we recognize today would be unfamiliar. The Commission has become neither the federal executive for which proponents of a United States of Europe wished, nor the technocratic *Commissariat du Plan* which many of its French designers envisaged, setting the agenda to which national governments respond. The popular movements, Europe-wide interest groups and political parties which the early enthusiasts for European union hoped would spring up once the initial structures were in place, to provide support for the central institutions in their struggles with national governments, are still shadowy, limited in their activities, and largely ancillary to their national components.[4] It has been national governments themselves which have borne the burden of formal integration. The Commission has played an active but ancillary role, building coalitions with key governments, while private groups seize the initiative intermittently. The Community system, as Wolfgang Wessels describes it, has become 'a golden triangle of Community civil servants, national civil servants and interest groups ... based on elite interactions, trust and reputation, by people whose loyalties remain primarily national but modify their expectations and behaviour to hold this highly valued system together'.[5]

Nor is the Community the sole or exclusive formal institution of core Europe. Around it have gathered other networks of intergovernmental cooperation, with varying memberships and diverse agendas, creating a diffuse set of formal structures with overlapping boundaries and competences alongside the diffuse informal development of a common European economic and social space. Among these networks are European Political Cooperation, Western European Union, the developing structures of EC-EFTA cooperation, the Council of Europe, the European Space Agency, and so on.

Within that dense policy space some players are clearly more important than others, and some provide disproportionate contributions to the public goods. West Germany, France and Britain contribute between them some 75% of Western Europe's defence expenditure within the Atlantic Alliance. Throughout the late 1980s the same three countries were net contributors to the Community budget, against nine (richer and poorer) net beneficiaries. West Germany and France in many ways recouped their contribution through the disproportionate influence their governments exercised over Western Europe's political agenda; Britain's influence was less consistently exercised. The temptation for these major players to bypass the inhibiting multilateral institutions of Brussels and operate directly with each other and through *ad hoc* arrangements has been evident, most of all in the extension of West European cooperation into the defence and security spheres and in global economic coordination with the USA and Japan.

But the centrality of the Community over the various *ad hoc* intergovernmental initiatives, sub-systems and alternative organizations and groupings is also clear.[6] The convergence first of European Political Cooperation and then of Western European Union towards the Brussels institutions reinforces the dominance of a common style and a common set of central actors, operating inside and outside the legal framework of the Community Treaties so far established: a 'Community system', in effect, based on shared understandings about rules and principles.[7] French, German and British approaches to the management of global political and economic issues shifted during the 1980s back from the Summits of the Group of 7 to the West European framework as the basis from which to concert relations with the USA, Japan – and the socialist countries. It is precisely because there is a degree of consensus about the character of the political regime and its broad rules – about the relationship between public authorities and the private sphere, about the role (and regulation) of markets, about the foreign policy and security framework within which to operate – that the actors can focus their attention on bargaining over more limited issues, and that informal integration can spread so easily across the space thus defined. The controversies which divided most of the governments of the EC at the end of the 1980s were about the closer definition of these broad economic, social and political rules: the limits to government support for industry in a market economy, the extent to which considerations of social policy should shape the regulation of market forces, the appropriate role of monetary policy and of macro-economic coordination in the management of the integrated European economy.[8] The rhetoric of the British Conservative government challenged a number of the underlying assumptions around which its partners were converging; but considerations of political and economic interest nevertheless pressed the British cabinet to accede to Community rules once a broad agreement emerged among the other major governments, however hard British representatives had argued for a different emphasis.

The East European countries, in contrast, lacked any comparable consensus on political, economic or social regimes; their alliance leader had enforced a set of common rules which had prevented informal economic or social integration and contributed to domestic political and economic failure. They were drawn towards the West European 'model' at the end of the 1980s both because of its evident 'success' and because there appeared to be no acceptable alternative on offer.[9] The pressure for convergence of East European countries on West European rules was strengthened by the choice of the EC Commission as the coordinator of Western economic assistance to Eastern Europe: a choice made with strong American support by the seven-nation 'Western' summit in June 1989. The Community, with its rules and decision-making procedures, thus seems on the point of extending its influence and authority eastwards, as it has already done northwards and southwards: the West European model spreading across Eastern Europe, as the nineteenth-century industrial revolution – and the eighteenth-century Enlightenment – spread from west to east.

If the Community and its institutions sustain their current momentum through to the 'completion' of the 1992 programme, the years 1985–93 will have replaced 1958–65 as the longest continuous period of institutional advance in the peaks and troughs of formal European integration. But the partial bargain represented by the 1992 programme leaves many aspects of the future structure of European cooperation unresolved. The underlying political issues of legitimacy and identity remain unsettled. The pressures from peripheral Europe for privileged access to the core, through Community enlargement or new forms of association, are increasing and thus raising expectations which will be difficult to satisfy. The dynamics of global economic and political change will continue to sweep over and around Western Europe, posing new problems for

100

European policy-makers and their so-far established structure of institutions and rules.

European integration, global integration

The integration of Western Europe, as has been argued throughout this essay, has been shaped as much by the international environment in which it grew as by its own internal dynamics. The Soviet threat and the American security framework set the context for the initial enterprise as much as did the bitter experience and aftermath of World War II. Turbulent developments in transatlantic relations and the international economy did much to defeat the confident plans of the 1969–70 *relance*. Concern with the pace of Japanese technological advance, and with the impact on European security interests of the shifting preoccupations of successive US administrations, launched the initiatives of the early 1980s. The Community system may be more firmly established in the 1990s; but it can still be shaken or strengthened by developments outside the European region – and by developments in global security, as well as in the global economy.

The stability of the Atlantic security framework enabled the governments of Western Europe to leave the issue of military integration to one side for an extended period, after the traumatic failure of the initiative for a European Defence Community in 1954.[10] Developments during the 1980s, however, well before the remarkable events of late 1989, had created 'a consensus in West European countries from right to left that a European security identity is desirable and that it should find an institutional expression'. This expression would come about through the revival and enlargement of Western European Union, through closer Franco-German military and security cooperation, and through governmental and industrial initiatives in military procurement.[11] The apparently rapid decline of the Soviet threat in 1989, together with prospects for major progress towards reductions in troop levels in central Europe and the likelihood of substantial reductions in American forces in Europe, sharply altered the context within which any further progress might be made towards West European integration in this field. Alternative threats to West European security which neither the United States nor the Soviet Union saw as their primary responsibility could push Western Europe's governments closer together, whether they came from Europe's southern or south-eastern periphery, or from the Middle East. Lower levels of perceived threat, conversely, would allow West Europeans to slow down the pace of integration.

The relationship between European regional integration and the American-led global economy was from the outset a matter of some ambivalence. It aimed both to enable the countries of Western Europe to play a fuller part within an open international economy, and (by discriminating in favour of regional partners against outsiders) to improve their position within that economy. The character of the global economy in the 1990s – the competitive challenge posed by other regions and countries, the open or closed quality of other markets, the structure of bargaining over global rules – will also affect how far the governments of Western Europe find themselves pushed together. Some, both in Europe and the United States, see the impetus behind the 1992 programme as deriving more from changes in the structure of the global economy than from changes within Western Europe itself.[12] If it is accepted that 'the reality of the closing years of this century is that the world of the democracies is increasingly a world of three centers of power' – that 'the Western economic system is now based on three regional systems, the North American free trade area, the European Community, and Japan' – then the formal institutions of the European Community are likely to play an increasingly central role in bargaining on behalf of their component governments with the other major players.[13]

The evolution of multinational enterprise towards global strategies may have outdated the European approach for which many of Europe's leading companies pressed in the early 1980s.[14] But the intricate relationships between companies, banks and governments in bargaining over access to one another's markets and over advantage in their own, which are apparent in North America and Japan as much as in Europe, suggest that the international economy is unlikely to be governed by market forces alone. They further suggest that business and national governments in Western Europe will therefore look to the European Community to protect and promote their interests on the global stage. The evolution of formal integration at the European level will be influenced not only by the degree of evolution of policy in other key economies, but also by the relative success or failure of European enterprises in responding to the challenge of their global competitors. 'The sense of belonging together and pursuing common objectives will in any case encourage trade and cooperation within a region more than vulnerable universal "integration" will, especially under the severe strains imposed by structural change.'[15] Thus questions of shared values, of community and identity are of importance in underpinning open markets, too.

It may be that 'neither economists nor politicians have fully grasped yet the new political economy of regional integration from which the 1992 programme derives its unexpected momentum as well as its international impact.'[16] In this new political economy the setting of international standards for new products and services, and the deregulation and reregulation of information and financial flows, are replacing the traditional issues of regulating trade in goods produced in different national economies. The impetus provided to progress in formal European integration in the 1980s by the informal progress of technical and economic change may well therefore carry the process further during the 1990s, as governments and the economic interests which lobby them respond to the convergent pressures of external competition and of technological innovation and its economic impact.

Nations, states, legitimacy and values

It has been argued above that the recovery of the centrality of the nation-state in Western Europe in the course of the 1950s was a temporary phenomenon rather than a return to a permanent or natural state of things. Social, technical and economic changes since then have undermined the autonomy of national governments within the confined geography and dense society and economy of Western Europe, forcing governments to pursue their objectives through common policies as interaction across borders takes economic and social behaviour beyond the control of any single national authority. The diffusion of market power and social networks has to an extent also diffused perceptions of community and identity; but these have not (as early proponents of European political integration hoped) been redirected towards any clearly recognized symbols and institutions of community at the European level.

The nineteenth-century nation-state in Western Europe successfully resolved the political problem of reconciling political community with the framework of law-making and enforcing power, thus providing a secure sense of identity and status for the former and legitimacy for the latter. Identity was strengthened by emphasizing the characteristics which distinguished members of each national community from outsiders; indeed by exaggerating the differences between the stereotypical members of each national community and their neighbours. Visible symbols of national unity reinforced the sense of solidarity. Heads of state were surrounded with pomp and ceremony; national monuments were erected; national parliaments and the judicial system were dignified with splendid buildings to reinforce their authority. Reinforcing symbolism with self-interest, every West European government also thought it wise to cement the loyalty of its citizens through redistributive tax policies and the beginnings of social welfare, to provide every citizen with a tangible sense of having a stake in the state.

The Community system has no comparable symbolic or financial resources at its disposal, nor has it any in prospect. Sources of legitimacy remain firmly at the national level, the visible involvement of national ministers in Community bargaining still providing much greater popular reassurance of accountability than the fledgling activities of the European parliament. Underneath successive arguments between the Community institutions and the national governments about the status of the President of the Commission, the creation of a European passport, the institutionalization of a European flag and the siting of the European parliament lie competing concerns over the importance of symbolic instruments in building a sense of shared community, and thus in reinforcing the legitimacy of the central institutions.[17]

The notion of community implies and involves shared commitment and shared benefits and sacrifices. To a limited but gradually increasing extent, the countries of core Western Europe have accepted this sense of community; with Community obligations largely accepted and implemented, with resources redistributed from Baden-Württemberg to Portugal and industrial adjustment tipping the balance from the Netherlands to Spain. The diffuse sense of identity and community which has grown up, as much from the processes of informal social integration (and from the reservoirs of common culture) as from the deliberate interventions of governments and Community institutions, has proved sufficient to support this degree of redistribution. The progressive expansion of the Community system and its role in the wider Europe will test this diffuse sense of community more rigorously – as textile workers in Yorkshire are asked to adjust to Polish or Romanian competition, as East European agricultural produce pushes into Western Europe's saturated markets, above all as taxpayers throughout Western Europe are asked to contribute in support of a lengthening list of *demandeurs*. The argument over redistribution within the formal structure of the European Community itself has not yet been fully addressed; its extension on any significant scale beyond the Community's boundaries will require careful political presentation to carry unqualified consent.

How far might such a sense of European community stretch, once the external boundaries which hemmed in Western Europe were removed? Western Europe, like its component nation-states before it, was defined partly in contra-distinction to those which were excluded: democratic Europe, against authoritarian Europe; market economy Europe, against command economy Europe; the West, against the East. There *are* exclusive definitions available for politicians to conjure up: Christianity against Islam, or Europeans against North Africans (as population pressures encourage illegal immigration) – potentially explosive in domestic politics as in external relations, but immensely attractive in emphasizing the distinction between insiders and outsiders. The problems of Russia and of south-eastern Europe, half in but half out of Europe's society and economy, now as in earlier periods of European history, may well prove the most difficult to resolve.

The political leaders of Western Europe cannot afford to leave to those around its periphery the definition of how far beyond its core areas the community – and perhaps eventually the Community – of Europe should extend. Political systems cannot operate without boundaries, nor markets without rules enforced within their limits; and boundaries necessarily exclude as well as include. Institutionalized Western Europe has operated with multiple boundaries for several decades, with layers of influence, commitment and obligation – and with shifting boundaries, as its core institutions have gone through successive enlargements. But a degree of convergence is observable, as rules become tighter and the trade-offs between benefits and sacrifices are made across an increasingly wide agenda. The choices which the EFTA countries face in seeking the fullest possible access to the benefits of Europe's common economic and social spaces will be presented in time to the Community's southern and eastern neighbours: to accept common rules, and common discrimination between insiders and outsiders, in return for the open access they seek. But how many such closely linked partners, over how broad and diverse an area, will the countries of core Europe wish to accept?

Direction and indirection: the importance of unintended consequences
Proactive formal integration set the framework of European rules and European institutions in the treaties of 1951 and 1957. Since then, however, Western Europe has moved forward through the interaction between partial political bargains and the undirected evolution of informal integration. The package agreed at the Hague summit of December 1969, for example, encouraged an explosion of agricultural expenditure, with unintended consequences for the Community's budgetary politics and political balance which forced further hard bargaining over budgetary rules a decade later. The creation of a customs union facilitated the development of integrated production across national boundaries, which in turn set off pressures for further adjustments in formal rules. The removal of all controls at the Community's internal frontiers was not fully understood as part of the initial bargain; the pressures which led to the inclusion of this specific objective within the Single European Act and the 1992 programme, and to the more radical measures of the Schengen Agreement, came from the accumulated weight of tourists, lorry-drivers, businessmen and law-enforcement agencies pushing against regulations which inhibited their new patterns of work and travel.

Idealists and constitutional lawyers may consider this untidy process of policy drift and coalition bargaining to be profoundly unsatisfactory. Far better in principle, faced with an evidently inefficient patchwork of institutions and implicit understandings, to design a new political system as a whole: to move, as it were, from the Articles of Confederation to a Philadelphia Convention, from the current collection of treaties, agreements and amendments to a new and lasting treaty of European union. Politicians are likely to answer that the system has worked well enough for their purposes, without too visibly or abruptly depriving existing national governments of authority or power.

The partial bargains struck – in 1969, much less successfully in

1972, over EMS in 1978, over the Single European Act and the 1992 programme in 1985 – have taken the member governments some distance further each time along the ill-defined road to a European union, and carried others along behind them. The countries of Community Europe have accumulated a broad agreement on complementary objectives and on the principles of mutual solidarity and diffuse reciprocity which govern their multilateral bargaining. They move reluctantly forward, in response to internal social and economic dynamics, to external pressures, and to the intended and unintended consequences of the rules they have already agreed. The intensity of their political, economic and social interaction is such that they are likely to move further, as they discover closer common interests and more pressing common problems, and negotiate new rules to promote and manage them. The movement is unlikely to be towards the design of any fixed or final political order. Instead, it will edge towards a confederal structure which will bear the load of policy-making which its participant governments recognize it requires. The peripheral countries of northern and southern Europe – and increasingly also of eastern Europe – will find themselves dragged along in the wake. That is, after all, the way that European integration has moved over the past 40 years, with many false dawns of euphoria and false nights of gloom; and, looking back, we can see a Europe transformed, partly by conscious design and partly by the accumulation of responses to undirected developments.

NOTES

Chapter 1

1 Fernand Braudel, in *Civilization and Capitalism, 15th-18th Century* (London: Collins, 1984), vol. 3, Chapter 1, distinguishes between economic, social and cultural time, emphasizing the importance of long-term trends in international economic development. In his earlier *The Mediterranean and the Mediterranean World in the Age of Philip II* (London: Collins, second revised edition 1972), vol. 1, p. 21, he divides 'historical time into geographical time, social time, and individual time'. My own conceptual divisions of time, cycles and trends draws on these and also on exchanges with Bela Kadar and John Roper about immediate events and underlying continuities in European developments.

2 *Declaration of the Heads of State and Government participating in the Meeting of the North Atlantic Council in Brussels, 29–30 May 1989,* para. 13; *Comprehensive Concept of Arms Control and Disarmament,* adopted by the same North Atlantic Council, para. 3 (Nato Information Service, Brussels).

3 Preamble to the Treaty establishing the European Coal and Steel Community (Treaty of Paris, 18 April 1951).

4 I am following Schumpeter's approach here, as updated and modified in such recent works as G. Dosi et al., *Technical Change and Economic Theory* (London: Pinter, 1988), and Rob van Tulder and Gerd Junne, *European Multinationals in Core Technologies* (Chichester and New York: Wiley, 1988).

5 To be published as William Wallace, ed., *The Dynamics of European Integration* (London: Pinter, 1990).

Chapter 2

1 Hugh Seton-Watson, 'What is Europe, Where is Europe?', eleventh Martin Wight Lecture, Royal Institute of International Affairs; reprinted in *Encounter*, July-August 1985, pp. 9–17.

2 The literature on mental maps is sparse. See, for instance, P. Gould and R. White, *Mental Maps* (Harmondsworth, Middlesex: Penguin, 1974); Alan K. Henrikson, 'The Geographical "Mental Maps" of American Foreign Policy-Makers', *International Political Science Review*, vol. 1, no. 4, 1980, pp. 495–530.

3 Timothy Garton Ash, *The Uses of Adversity* (Cambridge, England: Granta, 1989), p. 169.

4 Karl Polanyi, *Europe Today* (London: Workers' Education Trade Union Committee, 1937), p. 12.

5 Out of the vast literature on this theme in several languages, see, for example, Lord Gladwyn, *The European Idea* (London: New English Library, 1967); H. Brugmans, *L'Idée européenne, 1920–1970* (Brussels: De Tempel, 1970).

6 This habit had not entirely disappeared in the 1980s, even as the members of EFTA accommodated themselves to closer relations with the EC. Arriving with two German collaborators in this project and two French at a conference in Stockholm in December 1988, I was greeted with the comment that 'We are very glad to have so many participants from Europe.'

7 Lee Blessing, *A Walk in the Woods* (New York: Dramatist Play Services, 1988).

8 Contesting historical frames of reference were sharply evident during this transition; every Spaniard assumed that his or her country's major contributions to European development over the centuries were recalled and welcomed, while those from northern Europe were more conscious of Spain's separateness. I recall the Spanish minister responsible for negotiations with the European Community concluding a speech in Bruges in the summer of 1977 with a reference to the renewal of Spain's links with the Low Countries. 'Ah yes,' a Fleming on the platform remarked audibly, 'you used to burn people in the square.'

9 For these paragraphs I have drawn extensively on several essays in A. Rijksbaron et al., *Europe from a Cultural Perspective: Historiography and Perceptions* (The Hague: UPR, 1987).

10 Paul Kennedy, *The Rise and Fall of the Great Powers: Economic Change and Military Conflict from 1500 to 2000* (New York: Random

House, 1987), Chapters 2 and 3, provides a succinct summary of this argument. See also Anton De Porte, *Europe between the Superpowers: the Enduring Balance* (New Haven, CT: Yale University Press, 1979), Chapter 1. I have drawn on the broad sweep of De Porte's interpretation of the European balance throughout this chapter.

11 Sidney Pollard, *European Economic Integration, 1815–1870* (London: Thames and Hudson, 1974), Chapter 1.

12 J.M. Keynes, *The Economic Consequences of the Peace* (London: Macmillan, 1919), pp. 14–15. The conventional definition of 'Western' Europe in Britain and the Netherlands in this period was that it comprised the countries west of Germany. The German-speaking lands constituted central Europe, though one may also note the division within several foreign ministries between 'Northern' and 'Southern' Europe, along a line drawn between Germany and France, or between the Protestant and Teutonic north and the Catholic and Romance south.

13 Gladwyn, op. cit. (above, n. 5).

14 Thomas Mann, *Der Zauberberg*; quoted in W.H. Roobol, 'Europe in the Historiography between the World Wars', in *Europe from a Cultural Perspective* (cited above, n. 9), p. 52.

15 At a conference in early 1989 on EC-Austrian relations a senior Austrian exploded at the suggestion that there could be any comparison between Austria's claim to EC membership and the application already submitted by Turkey: 'but have you forgotten that we saved Europe from the Turks?' Mr Milosevic's Kosovo comment was quoted in the *Independent*, 24 June 1989: the Serbs, the argument goes, are again defending Christian Europe against Islamic fundamentalism, identifying the Albanians of the Kosovo region with the Turks who crushed the Serbian kingdom in 1389, and comparing their struggle with contemporary Iranian developments.

16 The attempt by a national curriculum working party in 1989 to define a British national history to be taught in state schools in England and Wales opened awkward questions of national identity and Anglo-Scottish relations. William Wallace, 'Why the history we are teaching is out of date', *Observer*, 22 October 1989.

17 Winston Churchill, *History of the English-Speaking Peoples* (London: Cassel, 1956).

18 Harold van B. Cleveland, *The Atlantic Idea and its European Rivals* (New York: McGraw-Hill/Council on Foreign Relations, 1966).

19 Louis Halle, *The Cold War as History* (London: Chatto and Windus, 1967), p. 242.

20 Gyula Szeku, *Forradalom Utan* (Budapest: Gondolat, 1983), p. 121. I am grateful to Lazlo Lang for the reference and the translation,

illustrating a mental map which shaped Hungarian intellectual and political reassertion in the 1980s.

21 Seton-Watson, op. cit. (above, n. 1), p. 14.

22 Jean Monnet, *Mémoires* (Paris: Fayard, 1976), pp. 316–23, 331–40. 'The core of six was accepted not as an ideal but as a transitional necessity in the knowledge, as Jean Monnet once said before the European Parliament, that the boundaries of the Six were not drawn up by the Six themselves but by those who were not yet willing to join them.' Max Kohnstamm, 'The European Tide', *Daedalus*, Winter 1966, p. 105. I have also consulted several of Monnet's former associates on this point.

23 Jeno Szücs, 'Three Historical Regions of Europe', in John Keane, ed., *Civil Society and the State* (London: Verso, 1988), p. 310, states that 'Around 1300, three quarters of Europe's population lived in the West', that is, in the Rhineland, France, Italy, south-western Germany, the Low Countries and the British Isles. The Danube basin and the north European plains were by contrast sparsely inhabited.

24 Allan M. Williams, *Western European Economy: a Geography of Post-War Development* (London: Hutchinson, 1987) pp. 82–5; Dudley Seers et al., *Underdeveloped Europe: Case-studies in Core-Periphery Relations* (Hassocks, Sussex: Harvester, 1979).

25 Pollard, op. cit. (above, n. 11).

26 Keynes, op. cit. (above, n. 12), p. 15.

27 Per Wijkman, 'Patterns of Production and Trade in Western Europe', in William Wallace, ed., *The Dynamics of European Integration* (London: Pinter, 1990), on which these paragraphs draw extensively.

28 Wijkman, op. cit.

29 Roberto Aliboni, 'The Mediterranean Dimension', and Richard Davy, 'The Central European Dimension', in Wallace, op. cit.

30 Elke Thiel, 'Patterns of Monetary Interdependence', in Wallace, op. cit.

31 On investment flows, see DeAnne Julius, *Global Companies and Public Policy: the Growing Challenge of Foreign Direct Investment*, Chatham House Papers (London: Pinter/Royal Institute of International Affairs, 1990).

32 Fred Bergsten, 'Economic Imbalances and World Politics', *Foreign Affairs*, Spring 1987, p. 776.

33 Pari Patel and Keith Pavitt, 'International Distribution and Determinants of Technological Activities', *Oxford Review of Economic Policy*, vol. 4, no. 4, p. 44.

34 William Walker and Philip Gummett, 'Britain and the European Armaments Market,' *International Affairs*, Summer 1989, p. 434.

35 Cited in Federico Romero, 'The Human Dimension: Cross-Border

Population Movements', in Wallace, op. cit., from which most of the information in these paragraphs is drawn.

36 Romero, op. cit.; citing in particular John Salt, 'High-Level Manpower Movements in Northwest Europe and the Role of Careers: an Explanatory Framework', in *International Migration Review*, Winter 1986, pp. 951–72.

37 Karl Deutsch, *Political Community and the North Atlantic Area*, (Princeton, NJ: Princeton University Press, 1957), pp. 18, 19.

38 Margaret Thatcher, speech to the College of Europe in Bruges, September 1988. She specifically mentioned the Poles, Hungarians and Czechs among the 'peoples who once enjoyed a full share of European culture, freedom and identity' (not entirely accurate in terms of history or of Western definitions of freedom) and included the USA (but not Russia) among the countries of 'European values'.

39 'A part of the Latin West which has fallen under Russian domination ... which lies geographically in the centre, culturally in the West and politically in the East.' Quoted in Karl Schlögel, *Die Mitte liegt Ostwärts* (Berlin: Corso, 1986), p. 12. Václav Havel's speech was reported in the *Guardian*, 26 January 1990.

40 The underlying debate about British national identity and its compatibility with European commitment which rumbled through British politics throughout the late 1980s made for the stiffest resistance to 'European' educational initiatives from London.

41 M.C. Brands, 'Europe Halved and United: From a Split Object to a Restored Cultural Identity?', in A. Rijksbaron et al., *Europe from a Cultural Perspective* (cited above, n. 9), p. 80.

42 Werner Weidenfeld, 'Was ist die Idee Europas?', in *Aus Politik und Zeitgeschichte*, June 1984, p. 8.

43 The quotation is from the NATO Summit Communiqué of 30 May 1989.

44 Harold van B. Cleveland, op. cit. (above, n. 18); Arnold Wolfers, 'Integration in the West: the Conflict of Perspectives', in Francis O. Wilcox and H. Field Haviland, Jr, eds., *The Atlantic Community: Progress and Prospects* (New York: Praeger, 1963), pp. 235–52.

45 Sergio Romano, 'Perceptions of Europe since 1945 in Italy', in *Europe from a Cultural Perspective* (cited above, n. 9), pp. 96–101, lays particular stress on this; it appears to have been strongest in the southern European countries from the 1940s to the present.

46 On the relevance of ideological hegemony in maintaining international regimes, see Robert O. Keohane, *After Hegemony: Cooperation and Discord in the World Political Economy* (Princeton, NJ: Princeton University Press, 1984), p. 137, following Gramsci's conceptual approach.

47 Robert Worcester, 'Attitudes to America, Americans and American
Foreign Policy: Europe', paper to 1988 IPSA Conference, Washington, DC, pp. 18–26.
48 Statement by the Eurogroup Defence Ministers, 7 June 1989.
49 Harmut Kaelble, *Auf dem Weg zu einer europäischen Gesellschaft*
(Munich: C.H. Beck, 1987).
50 On the impact of travel and contact on 'both cognitive and affective
attitude change', see Malcolm Hewstone, *Understanding Attitudes to
the European Community* (Cambridge, England: Cambridge University
Press, 1986), pp. 85–6.
51 *Eurobarometer* 25 (Brussels: Commission of the EC), June 1986.
52 Ernest Gellner, *Nations and Nationalism* (Oxford: Blackwell, 1983),
p. 86.
53 Most of these examples are taken from the section of the *Commission
Programme* for 1988 (Brussels: Commission of the EC, 1988) entitled
'Towards a European Society'.
54 Declaration of EFTA Heads of Government, Oslo, 15 March 1989,
para. 3.

Chapter 3

1 Alfred Grosser, *The Western Alliance: European-American Relations
since 1945* (London: Macmillan, 1978), p. 70.
2 Louis Halle, *The Cold War as History* (London: Chatto and Windus,
1967), Chapter 16, notes the gradual transformation of Western interpretations of Soviet behaviour into a new doctrine, formed of a series
of confused responses to local crises – with the Berlin crisis as the
point at which conviction of Soviet aggressive intent hardened into
accepted belief.
3 Alan S. Milward, *The Reconstruction of Western Europe 1945–51*
(London: Methuen, 1984), p. 96.
4 Max Beloff, *The United States and the Unity of Europe* (Washington,
DC: Brookings, 1963).
5 For FDI, I have drawn on work done by DeAnne Julius and Stephen
E. Thomsen at the Royal Institute of International Affairs.
6 Where not otherwise stated, figures in this chapter are drawn from
OECD and EC official publications.
7 There are no surveys of this rapidly moving field. I have drawn on the
work of Albert Bressand, and on a project led by Aubrey Silberston
for the RIIA on 'The Industrial Map of Europe'.

Chapter 4

1 This was Karl Deutsch's main intellectual preoccupation, both at the

national and at the international level. See *Nationalism and Social Communication* (New York: Wiley, 1953) and *Political Community and the North Atlantic Area* (Princeton, NJ: Princeton University Press, 1957).

2 Keith Robbins, *Nineteenth-Century Britain: England, Scotland, Wales, the Making of a Nation* (Oxford: Oxford University Press, 1989).

3 Ernst B. Haas, *The Uniting of Europe* (Stanford, CA: Stanford University Press, 1958), p. 13.

4 See, for example, Haas, op. cit., Chapter 11.

5 H. Hinsley, *Sovereignty* (London: New Thinker's Library, first edition, 1966), p. 214.

6 D.D. Raphael, *Adam Smith* (Oxford: Oxford University Press, 1985), p. 19. Adam Smith was part of the circle – and generation – of Scottish intellectuals who regarded themselves as 'north British'. The romantic movement reawoke Scottish self-consciousness, as it awoke national consciousness, and so nationalism, in other countries.

7 Gerald Newman, *The Rise of English Nationalism* (London: Weidenfeld, 1987).

8 Hugh Seton-Watson, *Nations and States* (London: Methuen, 1977), Chapters 1 and 3.

9 Ernest Gellner, *Nations and Nationalism* (Oxford: Blackwell, 1983), Chapter 3.

10 M. Panic, *National Management of the International Economy* (London: Macmillan, 1988), p. 142.

11 Keith Robbins, op. cit. (above, n. 2), p. 27. There were demonstrations in Gloucestershire against this 'alien' yardstick, imposed by outsiders from London and Birmingham.

12 Peter Kincaid, *The Rule of the Road* (New York: Greenwood Press, 1986), pp. 48–50.

13 Anthony H. Birch, *Nationalism and National Integration* (London: Unwin Hyman, 1989), p. 8.

14 Differences in individual, as well as in national, experiences under the impact of World War II also marked attitudes and behaviour in the decades that followed – in France as in Germany, in the Netherlands and Britain as in Italy. The divide between those British politicians of the 1960s and 1970s who had fought on the European continent – Heath, Carrington, Healey, for example – and those whose wartime experience had been of Anglo-American cooperation or work outside the military services – Gaitskell, Wilson, Thatcher – is striking.

15 Schumpeter's use of the term 'creative destruction' refers, of course, to the processes of *economic* change, but it seems equally appropriate to the emergence of new states out of the destruction of old empires.

16 Richard L. Merritt and Bruce M. Russett, eds., *From Nationalism to*

Global Community: Essays in Honour of Karl Deutsch (London: Allen and Unwin, 1981), p. 2. Coming to the United States in 1939, after the German occupation of the Sudetenland and then of the rest of Czechoslovakia, Deutsch toured the country as a speaker on behalf of the Free Czechoslovak Movement until the USA entered the war.

17 Foreword to Karl Polanyi, *The Great Transformation* (New York: Rinehart, 1957; first edition, 1944).

18 Enthusiasm for a United States of Europe was widespread in Washington between 1947 and 1950. John Foster Dulles was among its first supporters, declaring in a speech in January 1947 that it was 'the business of the United States to take the lead in reconstructing Europe on federal lines'. Resolutions supporting such a new entity were introduced into both houses of Congress in March, as part of the debate which led to the Marshall Plan. Max Beloff, *The United States and the Unity of Europe* (Washington, DC: Brookings, 1963), p. 20.

19 Karl Deutsch et al., *Political Community and the North Atlantic Area* (cited above, n. 1), p. 5.

20 Haas, *The Uniting of Europe* (cited above, n. 3), and Haas, *Beyond the Nation State* (Stanford, CA: Stanford University Press, 1964); Leon N. Lindberg, *The Political Dynamics of European Integration* (Stanford, CA: Stanford University Press, 1963).

21 London: Royal Institute of International Affairs, 1943. 'Functionalism' may be defined as the allocation of rule-making and -enforcing functions to the level of authority which is most appropriate to exercise those functions, rather than concentrating authority at any single level.

22 See also his *Nationalism and Social Communication* (cited above, n. 1).

23 See the discussion of Mitrany's ideas in Paul Taylor, *The Limits of European Integration* (London: Croom Helm, 1983), Chapter 1.

24 Lindberg, op. cit. (above, n. 20), p. 6; though Lindberg distinguishes his approach from that of Haas by not defining the end-point of this process as necessarily a federal state.

25 Lindberg, op. cit., p. 8.

26 Stanley Hoffmann, 'Obstinate or Obsolete? The Fate of the Nation State and the Case of Western Europe', *Daedalus*, no. 95, 1966, pp. 862–915.

27 Walker Connor, 'Nation-building or Nation-destroying?', in *World Politics*, April 1972, p. 352.

28 See, for example, Daniel Frei, 'Integrationsprozesse: theoretische Erkenntnisse und praktische Folgerungen', in Werner Weidenfeld, ed., *Die Identität Europas* (Bonn: Europa Union, 1985), pp. 113–31.

29 Deutsch et al., *Political Community and the North Atlantic Area* (cited above, n. 1), p. 4.

30 Ibid., loc. cit.

31 F. Machlup, *A History of Thought on Economic Integration* (London: Macmillan, 1977), p. 3.

32 New York: Carnegie Endowment for International Peace, 1950. See also Chapter 1 of Peter Robson, *The Economics of International Integration* (London: Allen and Unwin, third edition, 1987).

33 Charles P. Kindleberger, for example, was a member of the US State Department's Committee on Foreign Aid in 1947, and thus involved in constructing the Marshall Plan initiative. Economists associated with the GATT secretariat have differed over the years in their assessment of the interaction of regional and global economic integration from economists associated with the European Community and with most West European governments.

34 For an analysis of the ambiguities of the Spaak Report on the role of government in economic management and in redressing the imbalances of market operations, see Richard McAllister, 'The EEC Dimension: Intended and Unintended Consequences', in James Cornford, ed., *The Failure of the State* (London: Croom Helm, 1974).

35 Jacques Pelkmans, 'Economic Theory and the Impact of the Customs Union and the Common Market', unpublished paper, Tilburg University, June 1979.

36 Peter Robson, *The Economics of International Integration* (London: Allen and Unwin, third edition, 1987), p. 31. But see Tommaso Padoa-Schioppa et al., *Efficiency, Stability and Equity: a Strategy for the Evolution of the Economic System of the European Community* (Oxford: Oxford University Press, 1987).

37 Ralph C. Bryant, 'Intergovernmental Coordination of Economic Policies: an Interim Stocktaking', in *International Monetary Cooperation: Essays in Honor of Henry C. Wallich*, Princeton Essays in International Finance No. 169 (Princeton, NJ: Princeton University Press, 1987).

38 Joseph Schumpeter, *The Theory of Economic Development* (Cambridge, MA: Harvard University Press, 1934), p. 58.

39 Robert L. Heilbroner, *The Nature and Logic of Capitalism* (New York: Norton, 1985), p. 90.

40 Robert L. Gilpin, *The Political Economy of International Relations* (Princeton NJ: Princeton University Press, 1987), pp. 22–3; drawing in turn upon Polanyi, op. cit. (above, n. 17).

41 Christopher Freeman, 'The Third Kondratieff Wave: Age of Steel, Electrification and Imperialism'. Unpublished paper, Science Policy Research Unit, University of Sussex, September 1988.

42 Christopher Freeman and Luc Soete, *Information Technology and Employment: An Assessment* (Brighton, Sussex: Science Policy Research Unit, 1985), p. 23.

43 Albert Bressand, *Beyond Free Trade*, Prométhée Perspectives 8 (Paris: Prométhée, 1989), p. 7.

44 Patrick Minford, 'A Labour-Based Theory of International Trade', in John Black and Alastair I. MacBean, eds., *Causes of Changes in the Structure of International Trade, 1960–85* (London: Macmillan, 1989), pp. 196–7.

45 For a sceptical review of the extensive recent literature on strategic trade policy, the links between industrial organization and international trade, and the role of industrial policies, see Klaus Stegemann, 'Policy Rivalry among Industrial States: What Can We Learn from Models of Strategic Trade Policy?', *International Organization*, Winter 1989, pp. 73–97.

Chapter 5

1 Monnet's *Mémoires* make clear the very close involvement of American officials in all of the early moves towards formal integration within Western Europe. See also Robert Marjolin, *Memoirs 1911–1986* (London: Weidenfeld, 1989); Max Beloff, *The United States and the Unity of Europe* (Washington, DC: Brookings, 1963); Miriam Camps, *Britain and the European Community 1955–63* (Oxford: Oxford University Press, 1964).

2 On the pressure which the Johnson administration exerted, most of all on the German government, see Gregory Treverton, *The Dollar Drain and American Forces in Germany* (Athens, Ohio: Ohio University Press, 1978). On the Nixon administration's deliberate reopening of the terms of the postwar 'bargain', in 1971 and again in 1973, see William Wallace, 'Issue Linkage among Atlantic Governments', *International Affairs*, April 1976, pp. 163–79.

3 Robert O. Keohane, *After Hegemony* (Princeton, NJ: Princeton University Press, 1984), p. 137.

4 Quoted in Marjolin, op. cit. (above, n. 1), p. 213.

5 Max Kohnstamm, 'The European Tide', *Daedalus*, Winter 1966, p. 106.

6 Miriam Camps, Max Beloff, works cited above, n. 1.

7 The phrase is Joseph Joffe's, in 'Europe's American Pacifier', *Foreign Policy*, no. 54, Spring 1984, pp. 64–82.

8 Quoted in Jean Monnet, *Mémoires* (Paris: Fayard, 1976), p. 359.

9 Out of an extensive committed literature, see the survey by H. Brugmans, *L'Idée européenne* (Bruges: De Tempel, 1965).

10 Werner Weidenfeld, 'Was ist die Idee Europas?' in Weidenfeld, ed., *Die Identität Europas* (Bonn: Europa Union, 1985).
11 Monnet, op. cit. (above, n. 8), p. 350.
12 Stanley Hoffmann, 'No Trumps, no Luck, no Will: Gloomy Thoughts on Europe's Light,' in James Chase and Earl C. Ravenal, eds., *Atlantis Lost: US-European Relations after the Cold War* (New York: New York University, 1976). Theodore Lowi, 'Making Democracy Safe for the World', in James N. Rosenau, ed., *Domestic Sources of Foreign Policy* (New York: Free Press, 1987), pp. 295–332, argues that the nature of the USA's decentralized federal structure makes for a systemic tendency to oversell foreign policy proposals, necessary to carry them through a cumbersome network of legislative and executive bodies. It is similarly arguable that the decentralized and cumbersome structures of formal European integration make for the same systemic tendency.
13 The continuing relevance of wartime experience – by then a matter of recollection turning gradually into historical myth – was evident also in the attitude which the Norwegian government took to the Yugoslav application for association with EFTA in 1987–8. Its predisposition to find ways of accommodating the Yugoslavs, contrasting with the attitudes of the other Nordic EFTA governments, had its origins in the billeting of large numbers of Yugoslav prisoners in Norway during the war, when Norwegians braved the occupation regime to share food with their underfed working parties.
14 The history of these interactions is excellently summarized in Alfred Grosser, *The Western Alliance* (London: Macmillan, 1980), Chapter 7.
15 Uwe Kitzinger, *The Challenge of the Common Market* (Oxford: Oxford University Press, 1961), p. 144; Beloff, op. cit. (above, n. 1), p. 141.
16 The Action Committee for the United States of Europe, a body which had close relations with policy-makers in Washington, published a resolution in June 1962 declaring its objective to be 'the economic and political unification of Europe including the United Kingdom, and the establishment of a partnership between equals of Europe and the United States . . .': an aim which was echoed in President Kennedy's Interdependence Day speech the following month. See Max Kohnstamm, 'The European Tide', *Daedalus*, Winter 1966, p. 102.
17 *Declaration by the European Commission on the Occasion of the Achievement of the Customs Union, July 1st 1968*; reprinted in Michael Hodges, ed., *European Integration* (Harmondsworth, Middlesex:, Penguin, 1972).
18 The term *lourdeur* was adopted to describe the inefficiencies of the EC's decision-making processes by the 'Three Wise Men' report, *Report on European Institutions presented by the Committee of the Three to the European Council* (Luxembourg: EC, 1980).
19 Helen Wallace, 'Making Multilateralism Work: Institutionalized

Bargaining in Western Europe', in William Wallace, ed., *The Dynamics of European Integration* (London: Pinter, 1990).

20 Speech to Associated Press, New York, 15 April 1973 (the 'Year of Europe' speech). See also William Wallace, 'Issue Linkage among Atlantic Governments', *International Affairs*, April 1976, pp. 163–79.

21 Federico Romero, 'The Human Dimension: Cross-Border Population Movements', in Wallace, ed., op. cit.

22 Wolfgang Wessels, 'The Dynamics of Administrative Interactions: Towards a European System of Cooperative States', in Wallace, ed., op. cit.

23 The 4th Report of the House of Lords European Scrutiny Committee 1983–4, *Easing of Frontier Formalities*, does its best to reconcile the incompatible objectives of maintaining 'strict passport controls' and adjusting to a rising tide of movement across frontiers.

24 Michael Hodges, 'Industrial Policy: Hard Times or Great Expectations?', in Helen Wallace et al., *Policy-Making in the European Communities* (New York: Wiley, second edition, 1983). Susan Strange and Roger Tooze, eds., *The International Politics of Surplus Capacity* (London: Allen and Unwin, 1981).

25 William Wallace, 'European Defence Cooperation: the Reopening Debate', *Survival*, November/December 1984, pp. 251–61.

26 Alan Butt Philip, *Border Controls: Who Needs Them?*, RIIA Discussion Paper 19 (London: Royal Institute of International Affairs, 1989).

27 Helen Wallace, 'Making Multilateralism Work' (as n. 19).

28 Poul Schlüter, 'Europe – Heading towards the Year 2000', address to the America-European Community Association, London, 20 September 1988. In this speech Schlüter quoted Schumpeter on the 'creative destruction' of outworn practices, and suggested that the nation-state, 'the twin of the industrial society', was itself outworn.

29 W. Michael Blumenthal, 'The World Economy and Technological Change', *Foreign Affairs*, vol. 66, no. 3, 1988, p. 531.

30 Margaret Sharp and Claire Shearman, *European Technological Collaboration*, Chatham House Papers (London: Routledge/Royal Institute of International Affairs, 1987). Rob van Tulder and Gerd Junne, in *European Multinationals in Core Technologies* (Chichester and New York: Wiley, 1988), p. 251, see the ESPRIT programme as the creation of the twelve sponsoring European multinationals, and 'largely written by their representatives' rather than by the Commission.

31 Margaret Sharp, *European Technology: Does 1992 Matter?*, Policy Research Unit Papers in Science, Technology and Public Policy No. 19 (Brighton, Sussex: University of Sussex, 1989).

Notes

32 *A New Step for Europe: a Common Industrial and Research Area*,
memorandum submitted by the government of the French Republic to
the Council of the European Communities. Reprinted in *Europe
Documents*, Agence Europe, Brussels, 16 September 1983.
33 *Europe's Future in Space*, a joint policy report from five European
institutes of international affairs (London: Routledge/Royal Institute
of International Affairs, 1988), Chapter 4.
34 The quotation is from Susan Strange, 'Supranationals and the State',
in John A. Hall, ed., *States in History* (Oxford: Blackwell, 1986),
p. 298, but the sentiment was widespread in newspaper articles and
journals as the 1980s progressed.
35 Christopher Freeman and Carlota Perez, 'Structural Crises of Adjustment, Business Cycles and Investment Behaviour', in G. Dosi et al.,
Technical Change and Economic Theory (London: Pinter, 1988), p. 38.
36 Albert Bressand, *1992: the Global Challenge*, Prométhée Perspectives 9
(Paris: Prométhée, 1989), p. 4.
37 Tommaso Padoa-Schioppa et al., *Efficiency, Stability and Equity: a
Strategy for the Evolution of the Economic System of the European
Community* (Oxford: Oxford University Press, 1987). The quotation
from Delors is from the preface to this Commission-sponsored report.
See also Alexis Jacquemin, *The New Industrial Organization: Market
Forces and Strategic Behavior* (Cambridge, MA: MIT, 1987);
Jacquemin was an economic adviser in the EC Commission
throughout this period.

Chapter 6

1 Anton De Porte, *Europe between the Superpowers: the Enduring
Balance* (New Haven, CT: Yale University Press, 1979), p. xiii.
2 In these paragraphs I have drawn on a number of points made by
Pierre Hassner in a talk to the British International Studies Association conference at the University of Kent, 19 December 1989.
3 There have of course been several other partial initiatives for closer
Franco-British cooperation since World War II apart from those
which Monnet and his advisers promoted in the late 1940s, and the
briefly successful *entente* between Heath and Pompidou which took
Britain into the EC. The most disastrous was the 'Soames affair' of
1968–9, which the British interpreted as an attempt to drive a wedge
between London and Bonn. A minority of Macmillan's cabinet in
1960–62 favoured a closer political and technological partnership with
France to underpin Britain's approach to the EEC; but the majority
felt that the American and Commonwealth connections were more
important, and de Gaulle's stance did not make for easy accommoda-
tion between these two alternatives.

120

4 The rise of the 'Greens' across Western Europe during the 1980s, with active support and interaction between the various national groups, constitutes an interesting exception to this general observation. Those interested in comparison should note that American political parties remained loose confederations of state parties without any strong central structure until very recently.

5 Wolfgang Wessels, 'The Dynamics of Administrative Interaction: Towards a European System of Cooperative States', in William Wallace, ed., *The Dynamics of European Integration* (London: Pinter, 1990).

6 Philippe de Schouteete, 'The Community and its Sub-Systems', in Wallace, ed., op. cit.

7 Compare Robert O. Keohane, in *After Hegemony: Cooperation and Discord in the World Political Economy* (Princeton, NJ: Princeton University Press, 1984), p. 79, writing from an American perspective about the formation of international regimes among governments under conditions of intense interdependence: '*ad hoc* agreements in a dense policy space will tend to interfere with one another unless they are based on a common set of principles and rules.'

8 The Delors Report, para. 25, summarizes this broad consensus as 'the combination of a large degree of freedom for market behaviour and private economic initiative with public intervention in the provision of certain social services and public goods'. (*Report on Economic and Monetary Union in the European Community*, 12 April 1989, reprinted in *Europe Documents*, Brussels, 20 April 1989.)

9 I leave aside the controversial question of whether there is a significant difference between this West European model and the transatlantic model, as claimed not only by social democrats (and many Christian democrats) in Western Europe but also by 'reformers' in Eastern Europe. The partly symbolic arguments over the importance and content of the EC's Social Charter revolved around this issue, which may be seen as one of the many ways in which European policy-makers were attempting to define 'Europe' as an entity distinct from America.

10 There were also abortive discussions between the USA, France, Britain and Germany between 1958 and 1964 about the nuclear dimension of European defence, with proposals for an alliance 'Directorate' and for a nuclear 'Multi-Lateral Force'(MLF). If the British application for EEC membership in 1961–3 had been successful, the American administration would have put the issue of European security integration back onto the agenda; the collapse of the British application, and the intransigence of the position the French government thereafter adopted on NATO, left it as a submerged issue for a

further quarter-century. On the 1958–64 period, see Alfred Grosser, *The Western Alliance: European-American Relations since 1945* (London: Macmillan, 1980), Chapters 6 and 7.

11 Karl Kaiser, 'Directions of Change in the World Strategic Order', in *The Changing Strategic Landscape*, Adelphi Paper 237 (London: Brasseys/International Institute for Strategic Studies, 1989), p. 6.

12 See, for example, Wayne Sandholtz and John Zysman, '1992: Recasting the Global Bargain', *World Politics*, October 1989, pp. 95–128.

13 Laurence Eagleburger, in testimony to the Senate Foreign Relations Committee for confirmation as Deputy US Secretary of State, 15 March 1989 (US Information Service text); Karl Kaiser, op. cit. (above, n. 11), p. 8. See also Detlef Lorenz, 'Trends towards Regionalism in the World Economy', *Intereconomics*, March/April 1989, pp. 64–70.

14 For alternative views on this, see the concluding chapter of Rob van Tulder and Gerd Junne, *European Multinationals in Core Technologies* (Chichester and New York: Wiley, 1988), and Kenichi Ohmae, *Triad Power: the Coming Shape of Global Competition* (New York: Macmillan, 1985).

15 Detlef Lorenz, op. cit. (above, n. 13), p. 68.

16 Albert Bressand, *1992: the Global Challenge*, Prométhée Perspectives 9 (Paris: Prométhée, 1989) p. 13.

17 The emergence of the Community 'logo' in the late 1980s provides a good example of the ambiguities of the process. A proposal formally to adopt a Community flag would have aroused controversy far greater than that which had erupted over the principle – and design – of the Community passport, requiring heads of government to approve it specifically. The Community logo, far less threatening, was adopted on the proposal of the Commission by the Committee of Permanent Representatives. Once adopted, it was of course used on flags – but these lacked official status. The design used was a close derivation of the Council of Europe's symbolic circle of stars, with a smaller number of stars: another example of the EC invading the Council of Europe's sphere.

CHATHAM HOUSE PAPERS

General Series Editor: William Wallace
West European Programme Director: Helen Wallace

The Royal Institute of International Affairs, at Chatham House in London, has provided an impartial forum for discussion and debate on current international issues for some 70 years. Its resident research fellows, specialized information resources, and range of publications, conferences, and meetings span the fields of international politics, economics, and security. The Institute is independent of government.

Chatham House Papers are short monographs on current policy problems which have been commissioned by the RIIA. In preparing the papers, authors are advised by a study group of experts convened by the RIIA, and publication of a paper indicates that the Institute regards it as an authoritative contribution to the public debate. The Institute does not, however, hold opinions of its own; the views expressed in this publication are the responsibility of the author.

Related titles

The New Eastern Europe: Western Responses
J. M. C. Rollo
with Judy Batt, Brigitte Granville and Neil Malcolm

With this Chatham House Paper, published in April 1990, the Royal Institute of International Affairs makes its first major contribution to the fast-moving debate on Western policy responses to political and economic reform in the East. Concentrating on East Germany, Poland, Hungary and Czechoslovakia, the paper looks at the process of moving from a command economy to a market-oriented economy, and reviews the constraints faced by these countries in making such a transition (political, legal, managerial and structural). The aim of the study is to provide a framework in which to evaluate the appropriateness of the various actual and potential responses available to Western policy-makers. It thus attempts to specify those tendencies and processes that the West should encourage, to analyse the constraints in the West, and to identify the scope for division of labour among Western countries and groupings.

Financing the European Community
Michael Shackleton

The operation and structure of collective revenue and expenditure are always the subject of lively debate in the European Community. Over the years there have been intense arguments and complex solutions regarding both institutional procedures and substantive policy. In February 1988 agreement was reached on the so-called Delors package, which sets the framework for the EC budget over the longer term. This agreement made important innovations with regard to the level of agricultural expenditure, spending on other policies and the development of own resources. Subsequent decisions altered the institutional arrangements for managing the EC budget. This Chatham House Paper examines the implementation of these decisions and assesses the implications for the future financing of the EC.

Forthcoming book

The Dynamics of European Integration
edited by William Wallace

Europe has been reshaped over the past fifty years by war, by the structure of postwar alliances and institutions, by economic developments, social movement and techno-logical change. This volume, with chapters contributed by specialists from a wide range of disciplines and countries, examines the different dimensions of European integration. It assesses economic, technical and social trends, administrative inter-action, the role of law, and the establishment of stable patterns of negotiation and bargaining, and traces the consolidation of a core area of integrated economies and societies, which draw their neighbours to the north, south and east towards them.

RIIA/PINTER PUBLISHERS